ARTISAN
PIZZA

TO MAKE PERFECTLY AT HOME

GIUSEPPE MASCOLI
& BRIDGET HUGO

Kyle Books

CONTENTS

INTRODUCTION

When you find yourself eating in a Neopolitan pizzeria watching the skilled artisans working with flour, water and a few local ingredients, you are the latest in a very long line of customers. Pizza is the ultimate delicious, fast, affordable meal – one that was enjoyed by our ancestors in Ancient Greece and Persia. Archeological evidence found in Pompeii also shows that, in the 1st century AD, round-shaped flatbreads, cooked with rosemary, oil, garlic, cheese and anchovies, were being made in a wood-fired oven by a local baker, Podiscus Pricus, who sold them on a street near the Forum. A smaller oven, 120cm in diameter, dating from the 2nd century AD, has also been discovered in the Greco-Roman market area of Naples. Less than a quarter of the size of the Pompeian one, it is not ideal for bread, but is perfect for pizza. Located in the retail area of the town, in what today would be called the high street, the 'pizzas' made here, like those in Pompeii, were sold as street food.

Pizza remained solely street food until the late 18th century. Port'Alba, which began selling pizzas in Naples in 1787, added an interior seating area in 1830, becoming the first 'pizzeria'. Alexander Dumas ate there in 1835, noting that, 'in Naples, pizza is flavoured with oil, lard, tallow, cheese, tomato, or anchovies'. With the exception of tomato, these are the same ingredients that were being used 2,000 years earlier. Today, Port'Alba still operates on the same premises and continues to follow the same successful business plan.

Inevitably, in the 20th century, pizza fell victim to the fast food trend. What is too often offered on the high street today is far more corporate and industrial than local. Long fermentation has been abandoned for a fast-developing product. Dough is centrally produced, mechanically divided and frozen. The sourcing of the ingredients is globalised. Processed cheeses have taken the place of the short-lasting but long-tasting *fior di latte* or mozzarella. Skilled artisans have been replaced by semi-skilled labourers opening defrosted dough into a pan. Occasionally, 'entertainers' are hired to spin the dough in the air (something you will never see in Naples) to deceive the customers about the true nature of their operation.

Supermarkets also stack their shelves with pre-cooked pizzas topped with globally sourced ingredients of uncertain provenance. The collapse of trading barriers between countries has furthered the rush for cheaper products. In this situation the customer is ever more removed from the producer, the retailer and the stove.

Franco Manca was built on the belief that, although there are many ways of eating, to be truly enjoyed food needs to be made with integrity and with authentic ingredients. When we opened the first Franco Manca restaurant in Brixton Market in 2008, we were fighting against the tide. Between 1985 and 1989, it had been a pizzeria owned by Franco Pensa, and was called simply Franco. A legendary place, loved by the locals and mentioned in a number of books, including Geoff Dyer's *The Colour of Memory*, we were determined to honour its legacy. So we decided to call it Franco *Manca*. A common Italian surname, Manca also means 'missing', so Franco Manca means 'missing Franco' or 'Franco is missing'.

We had a wood oven built by one of the great Neapolitan artisans, Mastro Ciccio, and we trained local producers to make our mozzarella with Albino Scalizzitti, an artisan cheese maker from the Molise region. We sourced ingredients locally, and trained *pizzaioli* to master the ancient art of the Neapolitan oven. Our aim was to restore the reputation of the wonderful product that is pizza, and mend the injured 'mouth' of the consumer. Most people encouraged us. Others were sceptical, telling us 'the public will not understand the difference'. Fortunately for us, they did.

This book has exactly the same ethos as the Franco Manca restaurants and, like them, is an attempt to snatch pizzas from the jaws of globalisation. We want to encourage you to go back to the stove and the oven. The first and main principle is simple: know your products, your sources and what you are eating.

Engage, knead, think, bake and enjoy!

ESSENTIALS

Before you start, there are a few things you need
to consider, and a few things you may need to buy.
Whereas recipes are like still images of a moving
life – always an incomplete means to convey what
one has in mind – many cooking basics can be
measured as objects or used as rules.

Our main aim is to inspire and help, not to dictate.
Our descriptions are preliminary indications, whereafter
your own close encounters will fill out a much larger,
personal picture.

In this section you will find a few keys. Which doors
they unlock, or rooms they reveal, remains to be seen!

EQUIPMENT

BOWL

Our dough recipes feed 4 and make under 1kg of dough, so a 2-litre ceramic bowl is perfect.

Traditionally, pizza dough was mixed in a *madia*, a rectangular, hardwood container, usually made of beech wood.

ROLLING PIN

Pizzas are traditionally stretched by hand, but if you are inexperienced you may prefer to use a rolling pin. The best ones have no handles and are made of a hard wood, such as pear or cherry, but they always need to be 40–50cm long and 5–8cm in diameter. The wood has to be very well seasoned or it will warp.

SCALES

Having scales is highly recommended, especially for dough-making, where all your measurements need to be precise, but especially your liquid ones (ie. water). The best are balancing scales, as they do not break and do not require electricity. Digital scales are good too.

CONTAINERS

Whilst proving, dough balls are usually stored in beech wood boxes 6–8cm deep. You can make one for yourself to fit your fridge. You can also buy professional plastic pizza box trays, but even the smallest of these is quite large.

Hard wood is best as good pizza dough is very hydrated and the wood helps absorb moisture from the dough balls, which sweat as they develop.

Plastic is not as good but, if your container has a lid, provides decent insulation. The easiest alternative is a deep baking tray, though being metal, it offers poor insulation. If you go for this option, it is important to cover the balls with a damp cloth or thin towel. Make sure that whatever you use is large enough to tuck under the bottom of the tray to create a bit of tension so the cloth does not collapse onto the dough balls and stick. If you use clingfilm, brush it with oil first.

PIZZA STONE

In our experience, most domestic ovens fail to reach a sufficiently high temperature to make using a pizza stone worthwhile – it rarely becomes hot enough. This is not to say you should not try it. If you use a stone, you will also need a peel (a long-handled, spade-like tool) to move the pizza in and out of the oven.

IRON PAN

The baked pizzas in this book are all made using an iron pan. The dough is started on the hob and then, after the toppings are added, it is moved inside the oven or under a grill to finish. A suitable iron pan – 26cm in diameter - is easy to come by, not expensive and will last a lifetime. However, even this simple piece of equipment needs maintaining, so always dry thoroughly after cleaning and oil it immediately, or else it will rust. If it does start to rust, place it on the heat and rub it with oiled kitchen paper until the rust is removed.

If you already have a pan but of a different size, you can adapt the size of your dough balls to fit - herein lies another good argument for having scales!

BAKING TRAY

The dough recipe for tray pizza fits either a regular-sized baking tray (40 x 27 x 2cm), or two smaller trays (18 x 32cm). They need not be non-stick as you oil them anyway before baking.

DEEP—FAT FRYER

Pizza can be fried in a deep pot or in a deep-fat fryer if you have one.

THERMOMETER

A household or catering thermometer is essential for the novice pizza-maker, as we'll explain in the instructions for making dough. If you are deep-frying, an immersion thermometer is also useful.

DOUGH SCRAPER

This has either a plastic or wooden handle and a sharp metal edge. It's used not only to cut the dough and scrape clean the pizza tray, but also to lift the balls out of the dough tray.

SPOONS

A large metal spoon will help you to measure the sauce as well as spread it onto the pizza. Other standard measuring spoons such as a teaspoon and dessertspoon, and a measuring jug, will also come in handy.

DOUGH

There is no secret to a dough recipe – it is flour, water and salt... and yet each of these elements is key.

WATER

Water and flour have a vital relationship, as the amount of water you need in the mix depends on the type of flour you use. A strong flour absorbs more water and results in a stiff dough that makes for a hard and crispy crust. If you want a chewy dough with a lighter crust, it is best to use more water with a weaker flour, which will give you a more elastic dough.

FLOUR

The best is always stone-milled and made by humans rather than machines. It needs to be stored somewhere neither too wet nor too dry and, ideally, should be used within 6 months.

We use strong flour for our basic recipe. Stone-milled is preferable, but the really important thing is that it has not been bleached as this means it is free of chemicals, more nutritious and superior in taste. In Italy and France, flours are classified by their ash content, which means the amount of bran (the outer layer of the kernel of wheat) left after the milling process. Classification starts with the highest content (wholemeal = 2) going down to 1, 0 and 00. The best flour for pizza is 1 or 0 (although you could use a 2 if you want a more wholemeal taste and a 00 for a very white pizza).

Stone-milled flour is the best for making pizza at home and tends to be either 1 or 0, even when described as a 'strong white' flour. It will generally have an ash content of between 0.60 and 0.80%.

Protein (or gluten) is also key as this is what gives the dough good elasticity and robustness. The ideal content is about 12-13% and you can blend two flours (say a strong bread flour that is 15% with a plain flour that is 9% protein) to get the ideal 50:50 blend.

SALT

Salt is not simply a matter of taste, as it has its own chemical attributes and will affect the absorption of water and also the bacterial action in sourdough recipes. In general, salt content in pizza recipes ranges from 20g to 45g per kg of flour used, depending on the toppings.

The pizzerias in Naples that serve only Margherita and Marinara tend to use a lot of salt in their dough and no salt in their topping as this enhances the flavour of the pizza. (Tomato sauce also keeps better if it has no salt in it.) On the other hand, for a Pepperoni pizza, you would use less salt in the dough to counterbalance the salty sausage. In this book, as a rule of thumb, we use 25g of salt per kg of flour.

YEAST

Fresh and dry yeast are fairly interchangeable. Dry yeast powder is easier to come by and easier to use, so we use this in our recipes here. However, many people love the smell of fresh yeast as it activates and if this is your preferred method, go right ahead. You will need 30g of fresh yeast for every 10g of dry when substituting.

SOURDOUGH STARTER

This is a 'living food' of flour and water that contains yeast-producing bacteria collected from the air. The result is a culture, similar to yogurt (although the bacteria are of a different sort). Once you have the right bacteria, continue to feed the colony with flour and water.

These days, many people enjoy the practice of starting and maintaining a sourdough culture and, although an ongoing activity (a little like having a pet) a relationship develops, which makes the responsibility worthwhile.

In southern Italy the starter ('criscito' or levata) is often passed around a small village as one family will bake on Saturday and another mid-week.

FERMENTATION

The length of the fermentation is more relevant than whether you are making a yeast or sourdough pizza. A long fermentation will transform the starch into noble sugars and work through the proteins, making a much more digestible, and better tasting, pizza. It does mean preparing the dough roughly 24 hours in advance but you can make up a batch of dough to freeze for future use. If doing this, follow the dough recipe for baked pizzas right up until the product is shaped, and then freeze the bases.

TEMPERATURE

Temperature is very important when making pizza dough as ideally, the water, flour and ambient temperature should all be 18–20°C. In the absence of a thermometer, your aim is for water to be warm to the touch, but not at all hot. If your room temperature is very hot, you can use cold water. If very cold, you will need to use warm water and add a little more yeast or starter to the recipe – but no more than 30% more.

PROPORTIONS

At Franco Manca we make a very hydrated dough that, when baked in the extreme heat of traditional, wood-fired brick ovens, produces a juicy pizza with a crust textured with air bubbles and puffed up – the proverbial Neapolitan cornicione. However, we understand that making pizza in a home kitchen is different and therefore we have adapted our recipe so you can achieve the best results in that setting.

The recipes here makes a dough that is moist and flexible but not too difficult to handle. The aim is to use as much water as possible but if you find the dough unmanageable, slightly reduce the quantity of water.

FRANCO MANCA SOURDOUGH

At Franco Manca we only use sourdough because it adds an extra dimension to the taste. For the same reason, we always give it a long 24-hour fermentation. This method ensures good texture, great taste and added nutritional values.

THE FOLLOWING DOUGH RECIPES MAKE ROUGHLY ENOUGH TO FEED 4, EITHER 4 PIZZAS BAKED IN A PAN, OR 1 TRAY PIZZA (ENOUGH TO FEED 4). IF YOU WANT TO MAKE LARGER PIZZAS (USING A PEEL AND A PIZZA STONE) OR IF YOU HAVE MORE MOUTHS TO FEED, SIMPLY INCREASE THE QUANTITY OF DOUGH.

DOUGH I

FOR BAKED & FRIED PIZZAS

This dough will take about 16-18 hours to develop, so is ideal for making in the late evening for an early supper the following night. You can also make the dough in the morning for use in the evening by adding 20% more yeast. When working in this slow, natural time frame surprisingly little yeast is required (see tip opposite). Once you have made the recipe and you remember how much yeast you 'measured', it may be simpler to use just a pinch.

This is assuming you leave the dough in an ambient temperature of 20-23°C. If the temperature is colder (15-18°C) it will take a few hours longer.

YEAST VERSION	SOURDOUGH VERSION
MAKES 640G	MAKES 640G
250ml lukewarm (22°C) water	250ml lukewarm (22°C) water
0.2g dry yeast	30g starter
1 dessertspoon olive oil	8g olive oil
380g flour	380g flour
10g salt	10g salt

1. In a bowl or jug, measure out the water and add the yeast (or sourdough starter). Stir or whisk in, then add the olive oil.

2 Place the flour and salt in a large, 2-litre ceramic bowl and combine the ingredients with your fingertips.

3. Pour the liquid into the flour in a few stages, mixing each time with stiff fingers. (Note: use left hand for pouring water if you are right-handed.)

4. Work lightly, using only your fingers to draw the dough together and mop up all the flour. Avoid getting dough on the palm of your hand. Knead the dough a little with your knuckles.

5. Once the ingredients have roughly combined you can rest the dough. This gives the flour time to absorb the water and will make the dough easier to knead.

6. After 15 minutes, use your fingers and knuckles to knead the dough for about 5 minutes. Dipping your fingers in water will help keep the dough from sticking to your fingers while you do this.

7. Once kneaded, cover the bowl with clingfilm or a damp cloth and leave the dough to sit for 1 hour.

8. With a lightly oiled hand this time, fold the dough by drawing the four edges consecutively into the centre, and then pressing down on them. With the shape of your hands, form a large ball and then turn the mass over. Brush a bit more olive oil on top and cover the bowl again to store, making sure it's airtight.

9. Leave the dough in an ambient temperature of 20-23°C and in 16-18 hours, your dough will be ready to use. If the temperature is colder (15-18°C) it will take a little longer.

TIP

Dividing the yeast can seem tricky,
but it is not so. Usually a packet
of dry yeast is 7g. Divide this in
half on a smooth surface using
a plastic card or dough scraper
five times.

SHAPING BALLS

The baked and fried pizzas both start with a ball of dough that is opened (stretched) into shape: For pan baking, 160g balls will fit easily into the base of an iron pan. For *pizzette* (small, fried pizzas), cut the dough into 50g balls.

1. Tip the dough onto a floured surface and divide the developed dough mass into equal pieces with a dough cutter. Our dough recipe makes 640g, so that means dividing it by 4. Alternatively, you can weigh your balls on a set of scales.

2. Knock back the dough pieces by rolling them in a circle on a table until they form tight balls. When you do this, keep a tight grip around the edges of the ball with your fingertips while applying some pressure from the palm of your hand on top. You may want to practise, but do not overdo the shaping of each ball, as you will stress and tear the dough.

3. Place these on a floured surface in an airtight container or in a deep baking tray. If using a tray, drape a dampened tea towel over it, but be sure to tuck the edges of the cloth under the tray, so the rising dough does not stick to the sagging cloth. At normal temperatures (18°C) these balls will take up to 2 hours to prove. In a warm kitchen (24°C), 1 hour will be enough.

BAKING IN AN IRON PAN

I. Rub a 26cm iron pan with a little olive oil and place on the hob to get hot.

2. Sprinkle a little flour on your hands and on the table. Open a dough ball by flattening and stretching the dough gently with your fingers, or by rolling the dough with rolling pin.

3. Pick the pizza base up and gently, without tearing, stretch it a little further over your fists. Transfer the shaped pizza onto the hot pan.

4. Once the pizza starts to bubble and turn golden underneath it will be stiff enough to add toppings. After 3–4 minutes, transfer the pan to a 250°C oven (with the door shut) or place under a hot grill to finish. We find using a grill gives foolproof results.

FRYING

I. Divide the dough into 8 or 16 pieces. Shape these into round balls, cover and leave to rise for at least an hour in a warm place.

2. In a wide saucepan, warm 200ml groundnut oil (best) or vegetable oil (never olive oil) over a medium heat to reach a temperature of no more than 180°C (if you have a probe thermometer, this will be helpful).

3. Place a dough ball on a floured surface next to the stove. With your fingertips, flatten the ball into a disc, then pick this up and stretch it out a little, before placing in the hot oil.

4. Cook each pizzetta for a minute or so, then turn over. Do not overcook – if fried to a dark brown the flavour will be impaired. Place on absorbent paper to soak up the oil and then add toppings while warm.

STONE BAKING

We definitely prefer the pan-baking method as, if your oven is not hot enough or the stone you are using is not the best, the dough doesn't cook thoroughly underneath or rise enough on the stone. However, it is worth trying, and with a little experimenting, you can achieve satisfaction. Here's the method for giving it a try.

I. Turn the oven on to its highest setting and place a pizza stone on the highest rack to heat for at least 15 minutes after the oven has reached full temperature.

2. Sprinkle a little flour on the peel (see page 11) and open the dough ball onto it.

3. Follow the recipes for baked pizzas from the pages ahead. Using a peel, move the prepared pizza onto the stone and bake for about 8–10 minutes.

DOUGH 2

FOR TRAY-BAKED PIZZAS

The best tray pizzas are made with a very wet and elastic dough, based on a method using 'poolish' (an equal mix of flour and water with added yeast). This is made about 16 hours in advance of the dough. The total dough recipe here makes enough for 1 pizza (1kg) and is enough to feed 4.

The best way to mix this dough is to use an electric blender with a dough hook. If working without, be prepared to apply elbow grease.

FOR THE POOLISH	FOR THE DOUGH
400ml lukewarm (22°C) water	160g flour
400g flour	7g dry yeast
6g dry yeast	12g sugar
	16g salt
	2 tablespoons olive oil

NOTE: Make the poolish the day before you make pizza by combining all the ingredients in a bowl. Cover and set aside in the fridge for AT LEAST 16 hours and no longer than 48 hours.

1. In a large bowl, mix the flour, yeast and sugar into the poolish and combine. As it comes together, use the strength of your arm and stiff fingers to beat it for about 6 minutes. You might have to rest every few minutes! With a mixer this should take about 4 minutes. You are aiming for a smooth, elastic dough that starts to 'shine'.

2. Add the salt and oil and mix again until these ingredients are absorbed into the dough, then turn the mixture out into a lightly oiled bowl and 'rest' for 20 minutes.

3. Transfer the dough onto an oiled tray and fold into shape, following the dimensions of the tray you are using. Then turn it over, so the 'good' side is up.

4. Turn your oven on to its highest setting and place a rack on the middle shelf.

5. Stretch the dough towards the edges of the tray in 2 stages, resting for 10 minutes between each stretch.

When stretching the dough, try not to touch it on top, but use your finger tips from underneath the dough mass.

6. After the second stretch, add your toppings. If using tomato sauce, make sure it is spread right to the edges of the dough. If you are using olive oil, pour it into the palm of your hands and pat it lightly over the top of the dough, again making sure it touches the edges.

7. If the dough is deep (or the tray small) you can dimple the dough with your fingertips, making a focaccia-style deep pizza and adding more sauce or oil. If you have stretched the dough very thin, simply add the rest of your ingredients and seasonings.

8. Bake on the middle rack of your pre-heated oven for 12-14 minutes. If you have created a very thin pizza base, check for doneness after 10 minutes.

TOMATO

Good-quality tomatoes are key to a rich-tasting pizza sauce so try to source the best you can find. Fresh tomatoes have a short season in summer, anything between 6 weeks in temperate zones to 3 months in warmer climes. For the rest of the year, unless you've made your own passata, which we highly recommend, you are better off buying canned tomatoes.

PASSATA

When the best fresh tomatoes are used for passata, no further cooking is needed and the sauce can be used as-is. Depending on the juiciness of your tomatoes, different quantities of passata will be yielded. You should get about 1 litre of passata from every 5kg tomatoes.

a large shopping bag
   of San Marzano or
   plum tomatoes

a few basil leaves,
   torn

1. Sort through the tomatoes, cutting off any black parts and discarding any that are damaged. Wash well and steep in boiled water for 2–3 minutes, then drain in a colander.

2. Pass the tomatoes through a food mill, collecting the pulp, which is now ready to be bottled. Add a leaf of basil for extra flavour. Use sealable bottles (for example beer bottles with a crown) or jars with lids.

3. To sterilise the jars of passata place them, unsealed, in a deep pan and fill the pan with cold water, almost to the rims of the jars. Bring to the boil, then remove the pan from the heat and carefully seal. If you have a thermometer, you can take the pot off the boil when the water has reached 90˚C.

4. Your passata will keep for a year if stored in a cool, dark place.

BASIC SALSA

Without fresh tomatoes, you can make an on-the-spot sauce using either bought passata or canned tomatoes. (Italian products tend to be better – see Resources, page 124.) When buying cans, go for whole, peeled tomatoes instead of chopped, as they're better quality. The sauce will gain extra flavour if you reduce it slightly and add a little basil. We recommend you add garlic or chilli only to your pizzas (not to your sauce) as they do not complement all toppings, particularly in their raw state.

MAKES ENOUGH FOR 4 PIZZAS

240g (1 can) whole,
   peeled tomatoes

fine sea salt, to taste
fresh basil, torn

1. In a large bowl, squeeze the tomatoes hard through your fingers to crush.

2. If you are reducing your sauce, simmer in a pan over a low heat for 5 minutes. .

3. Add a few leaves of fresh basil and fine sea salt to taste. The flavour should all be in the tomatoes so be careful not to over-salt.

SALSA LARDIATA (CON SUGNA)

If you are after a richer tomato topping, this is a great variation you can use for both the passata and basic salsa. Either regular lard or a speciality cured lard (see page 71) will add flavour to the meaty tang of the reduced tomatoes, and the onion keeps the deal sweet.

MAKES 500ML

500g passata or fresh, juicy tomatoes peeled and chopped

40g lard or cured lard

100g onion

sea salt and freshly ground black pepper, to taste

1. On a chopping board, with heavy knife, chop the onion together with the (cured) lard, beating the latter into the onion with the blunt edge of the knife.

2. In a frying pan, season the crushed onion and sweat over a low heat until the onion has 'melted'.

3. Add the tomato, stir to combine and leave to simmer for at least 1 hour (the longer the better). Season to taste, being careful not to oversalt.

CHEESE

There are many ways to make pizzas without tomato, but few can imagine pizza without cheese, and mozzarella in particular. The other Italian cheeses used on pizza are ricotta, provolone and caciocavallo. However, there are many other cheeses you can try and, in recent years, there has been a great resurgence of artisan cheeses in Anglo-Saxon countries. The UK produces a number of amazing signature cheeses and at Franco Manca we make use of Montgomery Cheddar, Stichelton, Ogleshield and Colton Bassett Stilton, to name only a few.

Mozzarella

Mozzarella used for cooking is always *fior di latte*, or cow's milk mozzarella. Buffalo mozzarella is only ever added on top of a pizza after it has been baked. Proper *fior di latte* has either no or low pasteurisation, which means it will last no more than 3 days. Increasingly, small cheese makers outside Italy are making their own mozzarella. You can even buy a kit to make it yourself. At Franco Manca, we've trained a cheese maker in Somerset to make our mozzarella and also ricotta.

Ricotta

The better varieties of ricotta are firm and fairly dry, and we suggest thinning them slightly with milk, to make *crema di ricotta*. Shop-bought ricotta is usually already fairly soft.

Parmesan

If you are using Parmesan, use only Reggiano. Other Parmesans might cost less but are often tasteless and have a waxy texture.

Roquefort

If you need a blue cheese, you can never go wrong with Roquefort. Most countries, though, have their own varieties, so always experiment. The best ever will be the cheese one has found from a farmer one has met, if possible. As with all things in life, we are biased towards people we know, and rightly so.

Gruyère

Another variety of cheese good for some recipes is a Comté or Gruyère (Comté used to be Gruyère and, despite leaving the appelation, it still is). Of the Swiss and French Gruyères, the French is said to have less bite.

SMOKING YOUR OWN CHEESE

Smoked mozzarella adds a wonderful dimension to certain pizzas and we've included recipes on page 45, 65, 88, 105 and 121. It's very easy to smoke your own as you don't even need a proper smoker. Here's the method for making tea or straw-smoked mozzarella.

1 x 125g mozzarella ball
10g loose-leaf tea (preferably white or silver tea) or straw

1. Remove the mozzarella from its packaging, pat dry with kitchen paper and rest in the fridge for 12–24 hours until it dries out (it must be dry enough not to drip).

2. If you have a smoker, cold-smoke for 10 minutes with either tea or straw. If you don't have a smoker, place the mozzarella on a piece of wire mesh and place this in the oven on the top rack.

3. Scatter the tea or straw onto a baking tray and cover with foil, ensuring all the edges are sealed. If there are any tears, start again as otherwise your smoke will escape.

4. Place the baking tray on the stove and heat until it is very hot. This will trap a lot of smoke in the tray.

5. Carefully transfer the tray to the oven, remove the foil and immediately shut the oven door. Repeat the operation after 15 minutes, then leave the cheese for 20 minutes in the oven.

OILS & FATS

Oils and fats add an extra layer of flavour to pizzas, as do animal drippings. Olive oil is the traditional oil used and the best is made from olives that are not only free from insecticides and cold pressed, but also hand-picked. You can flavour olive oil very effectively with garlic, chilli or herbs (see page 58) and this makes both a wonderful pizza ingredient or optional condiment.

It is not necessary, though, to limit yourself to olive oil. Some of the best pizzerias in Naples use other vegetable oils - Pizzeria Michele uses soya seed oil. You could also use cold-pressed rapeseed oil, which has a wonderful colour, although it lacks the flavour of olive oil. Ground nut oil is also good.

If you roast a duck or goose you will end up with copious amounts of delicious fat. The same applies to pork fat. Many Neapolitan *pizzaioli* use the latter as a 'secret' ingredient to enhance the taste of their pizzas.

RENDERING LARD

This quantity of back fat will give you about 1.5kg of lard. After you have fried the fat, you will be left with soft pork scratchings. Mix these with 20g salt and 8g freshly ground black pepper and either vacuum pack or refrigerate in a sealed container.

2kg pork back fat, separated from the rind and cut into small cubes

1. Place the fat in a pan, cover with water and bring to a very low boil. Leave to simmer on a very low heat. As the water evaporates, the fat will start to melt. Do not allow the fat to colour.

2. When all the fat has melted and is still very hot, carefully drain through a sieve and pour into sterilised glass jars. Seal and store either in the fridge or a cool, dark place for up to 6 months.

PIZZAS

The recipes that follow show quantities per pizza, so multiply these by the number of people you plan to enjoy your pizzas with. The dough recipes are already calculated to make enough for 4 people, as it is not worth making less dough than this at a time.

Quality ingredients are important and the prep does require a certain amount of time – maintaining your sourdough starter and waiting for the fermentation of dough, for example – yet pizza making will still feel like a spontaneous and joyful event when it comes to the final bake off.

The selection of toppings and the preparation of some of these likewise requires a little forethought, but any time spent seeking out the best ingredients will bring rewards that utterly justify your efforts.

The Margherita is a benchmark pizza and provides the ultimate taste test for your raw materials of dough, tomato, olive oil and cheese. Make sure they're the best and you cannot go wrong. Use this recipe to test your skills and the quality of your principal ingredients before adventuring into the wonderful world of other toppings.

MARGHERITA BAKED OR TRAY

ingredients, per pizza

1 dough ball (see page 16),
   left to rise for
   1½ –2 hours OR
   dough 2 for tray pizzas
flour, for dusting

1 dessertspoon tomato
   sauce (see page 20)
1 dessertspoon olive oil
60g *mozzarella fior di
   latte*, torn into 5 chunks
4 basil leaves, torn, plus
   more to serve

Place a rack on the highest shelf of an oven and turn the grill to its highest setting. When hot, place a greased 26cm iron pan on the stovetop, set to medium heat.

Sprinkle a little flour over your hands and on the work surface and open the dough ball by flattening and stretching the dough with your fingers, or by rolling the dough with a rolling pin. Pick the pizza base up and gently stretch it a little further over your fists without tearing it. Drop this onto the hot pan, and allow it to start rising.

As soon as the dough firms up, spread the tomato sauce over the base with the back of a metal spoon. Drizzle with olive oil and distribute the basil and mozzarella on top.

Cook the pizza on top of the stove for about 3 minutes, then transfer the pan to the grill for a further 3–4 minutes.

Once ready, decorate with a little more basil and serve in one piece or sliced.

For the tray method
Follow the recipe instructions on page 19. The whole process will take about 90 minutes. Heat the oven to 260°C/gas mark 8 and stretch the dough to the edges of the tray. Be sure to spread your sauce right to the edges before adding toppings. The tray pizza dough serves 4, so quadruple the ingredient quantities. Bake for no less than 10 minutes.

INGREDIENT NOTE

A Margherita sometimes has a very small quantity of *crotonese* (a sheep's cheese from Calabria), which has a very strong but rounded taste. Another way to enhance the flavour, used by master *pizzaioli*, is to add a tablespoon of lard.

This is a bianca pizza – meaning the base is white (*bianco*), i.e. without a tomato sauce. Here, the base simply forms the bread accompaniment to what is essentially a cured meat and cheese salad. With such fresh ingredients, this is perfect for summer, served with lashings of good olive oil.

BRESAOLA, CHERRY TOMATOES & BUFFALO MOZZARELLA BAKED

ingredients, per pizza

1 dough ball (see page 16),
   left to rise for
   1½ –2 hours
flour, for dusting

1 dessertspoon extra virgin
   olive oil
5 cherry tomatoes, halved
a handful of rocket,
   washed
50g buffalo mozzarella,
   torn into 5 chunks
4 slices bresaola
freshly ground black
   pepper

Place a rack on the highest shelf of an oven and turn the grill to its highest setting. When hot, place a greased 26cm iron pan on the stovetop, set to medium heat.

Sprinkle a little flour over your hands and on the work surface and open the dough ball by flattening and stretching the dough with your fingers, or by rolling the dough with a rolling pin. Pick the pizza base up and gently stretch it a little further over your fists without tearing it. Drop this onto the hot pan, and allow it to start rising.

As soon as the dough firms up, drizzle the olive oil over the base.

Cook the pizza on top of the stove for about 3 minutes, then transfer the pan to the grill for a further 3–4 minutes.

Once ready, dress with all the ingredients in the order listed and finish with a couple of grinds of fresh black pepper.

INGREDIENT NOTE

See page 71 for how to make your own bresaola.
It also makes a great antipasto, simply dressed with
a squeeze of lemon, a drizzle of olive oil and a few
grinds of black pepper. Slice as thinly as possible.

Good pancetta is essential to this recipe so it might require a trip to your local butcher or deli (and ask for it to be sliced thinly). If you only have an average bacon to hand, we recommend you use good-quality cooked ham instead.

PANCETTA & AUBERGINE BAKED

ingredients, per pizza

1 dough ball (see page 16), left to rise for 1¹/₂ –2 hours

flour, for dusting

5 thin slices aubergine

1¹/₂ dessertspoons extra virgin olive oil

sea salt

4 dessertspoons tomato sauce (see page 20)

4 slices pancetta

60g *mozzarella fior di latte*, torn into 5 chunks

4 basil leaves, torn

a handful of rocket

Parmesan, grated (optional)

Place a rack on the highest shelf of an oven and turn the grill to its highest setting. When hot, place a greased 26cm iron pan on the stovetop, set to medium heat.

In a shallow pan, fry the aubergine in 1 dessertspoon olive oil until soft, golden and a little crispy. Season with salt to taste and set aside.

Sprinkle a little flour over your hands and on the work surface and open the dough ball by flattening and stretching the dough with your fingers, or by rolling the dough with a rolling pin. Pick the pizza base up and gently stretch it a little further over your fists without tearing it. Drop this onto the hot pan, and allow it to start rising.

As the dough firms up, spread the tomato sauce evenly over the base with the back of a metal spoon. Add the pancetta and aubergine, then drizzle with the remaining olive oil and scatter over the mozzarella and basil.

Cook the pizza on top of the stove for about 3 minutes, then transfer the pan to the grill for a further 3–4 minutes.

Once ready, dress with the rocket leaves and a little grated Parmesan won't hurt either, if you have it. Serve whole or in slices.

This simple pizza makes use of the softest mozzarella – 'burratina' – that takes the taste to such a distinct level of creaminess that it is best eaten uncooked. This simple topping is also great for small, fried pizzette (see page 116).

BURRATA PUGLIESE BAKED OR FRIED

ingredients, per pizza

1 dough ball (see page 16),
  left to rise for
  1½ –2 hours
flour, for dusting

1 dessertspoon extra virgin
  olive oil
5 cherry tomatoes, halved
80g burratina, torn into
  6 chunks
a handful of rocket,
  washed
freshly ground black
  pepper

Place a rack on the highest shelf of an oven and turn the grill to its highest setting. When hot, place a greased 26cm iron pan on the stovetop, set to medium heat.

Sprinkle a little flour over your hands and on the work surface and open the dough ball by flattening and stretching the dough with your fingers, or by rolling the dough with a rolling pin. Pick the pizza base up and gently stretch it a little further over your fists without tearing it. Drop this onto the hot pan, and allow it to start rising.

As soon as the dough firms up, drizzle the olive oil over the base.

Cook the pizza on top of the stove for about 3 minutes, then transfer the pan to the grill for a further 3–4 minutes.

Dress with all the ingredients in the order above, and finish with a couple of grinds of fresh black pepper.

For fried pizza, see the method on page 17

Pesto and potato are a common pairing in Italy as they are made from readily available garden ingredients. In fact, Genovese pasta recipes for pesto also usually include cooked potato. The garlic and herbs marry well with the creamy spuds, and the result is hearty yet simple.

PESTO WITH BAKED POTATO & PARMESAN BAKED

ingredients, per pizza

1 dough ball (see page 16),
    left to rise for
    1½ -2 hours
flour, for dusting

for the potato topping (makes enough for 4 baked pizzas)

320g Maris Piper potatoes,
    washed and cut into
    small wedges
1 dessertspoon plus
    1 teaspoon olive oil
    (or a little dripping)
1 teaspoon fine sea salt
½ medium onion,
    finely sliced
60g cherry tomatoes,
    halved

4 dessertspoons tomato
    sauce (see page 20)
3 teaspoons basil pesto
    (see page 34)
60g *mozzarella fior di latte*, torn into 5 chunks
Parmesan shavings
2 teaspoons extra virgin
    olive oil

Make the potato topping: Preheat the oven to 200°C/gas mark 4.

In a roasting pan, mix the potatoes with a dessertspoon of olive oil and sea salt and bake in the oven for about 40 minutes. Drain on kitchen paper.

In a heavy pan, sweat the onions in 1 teaspoon of oil (or a little dripping) over a very low heat until soft. Turn up the heat slightly and add the cherry tomatoes to the pan. When the ingredients start to caramelise and become sticky, add the baked potato wedges and turn off the heat. While the mixture cools, toss well.

Place a rack on the highest shelf of an oven and turn the grill to its highest setting. When hot, place a greased 26cm iron pan on the stovetop, set to medium heat.

Sprinkle a little flour over your hands and on the work surface and open the dough ball by flattening and stretching the dough with your fingers, or by rolling the dough with a rolling pin. Pick the pizza base up and gently stretch it a little further over your fists without tearing it. Drop this onto the hot pan, and allow it to start rising.

As soon as the dough firms up, spread the tomato sauce over the base with the back of a metal spoon. Distribute a quarter of the baked potato mixture on top and finish with the basil pesto and mozzarella.

Cook the pizza on top of the stove for about 3 minutes, then transfer the pan to the grill for a further 3–4 minutes.

Dress with the shaved Parmesan and a little more oil and serve in pieces or whole.

BASIL PESTO

PESTO DI BASILICO

Pesto is traditionally made with a mortar and pestle – ideally a stone mortar and a wooden pestle.

If you use a food processor, blend in the same order as given below. Genovese pesto has about half the quantity of oil given in this recipe, but is specifically for use with pasta. You can use Neapolitan, large-leaf basil with a bit of Greek basil, if you like.

MAKES 250ML

2–3 garlic cloves
1 teaspoon coarse sea salt
50g basil leaves
10g pine nuts or walnuts
200ml olive oil
30g Pecorino (or aged sheep's cheese), grated
70g Parmiggiano reggiano, grated

With a mortar and pestle, crush the garlic with half the salt. When well crushed, add the basil and the remaining salt. Rotating the pestle against the side of the mortar, keep crushing the pesto until the basil releases a green liquid. Add the pine nuts and keep crushing. If you use walnuts, use ones in the shell, as the shelled walnuts degenerate easily, acquiring a rancid aftertaste.

When all is well crushed, start adding the oil and the cheeses until you have an homogenous mix.

WILD GARLIC PESTO

AGLIO SELVATICO PESTO

In spring, you should be able to find plenty of garlic growing in the wild. However, it is also possible to cultivate some in a shady corner of your garden. This pesto is a wonderful way to enjoy it.

MAKES 200ML

2–3 garlic cloves
50g wild garlic greens
150ml olive oil
100g hard-aged Cheddar or sheep's cheese

Blend everything together, starting with the garlic and wild garlic greens and finishing with the cheese and the oil – either in a pestle and mortar or in a blender.

Good lamb makes a great alternative to cooked ham or cured meat as a pizza topping and combines well with a hard cheese like Pecorino. We find that children and anyone who is impartial to mozzarella are particularly fond of this pizza.

LAMB MINCE & PECORINO BAKED OR TRAY

ingredients, per pizza

1 dough ball (see page 16),
   left to rise for
   1½ –2 hours OR
   dough 2 for tray pizzas
flour, for dusting

4 dessertspoons tomato
   sauce (see page 20)
1 dessertspoon extra virgin
   olive oil
70g lamb mince (see
   below)
60g *mozzarella fior di
   latte*, torn into 5 chunks
4 basil leaves, torn
4 teaspoons Pecorino

for the lamb mince
   (makes enough
   for 4 baked pizzas)
1 tablespoon olive oil
300g lamb mince
1 teaspoon fine sea salt
1 garlic clove, peeled and
   crushed
a few mint leaves, finely
   chopped
1 dessertspoon grated
   Pecorino

Make the lamb mince: Heat the oil in a wide, shallow pan over a medium heat, then add all the ingredients and flash-fry briefly until the lamb turns slightly brown. (It will cook more thoroughly and crisp off slightly once on the pizza.)

Place a rack on the highest shelf of an oven and turn the grill to its highest setting. When hot, place a greased 26cm iron pan on the stovetop, set to medium heat.

Sprinkle a little flour over your hands and on the work surface and open the dough ball by flattening and stretching the dough with your fingers, or by rolling the dough with a rolling pin. Pick the pizza base up and gently stretch it a little further over your fists without tearing it. Drop this onto the hot pan, and allow it to start rising.

As soon the dough firms up, spread the tomato sauce over the base with the back of a metal spoon and drizzle the olive oil on top. Crumble a quarter of the lamb mince over the pizza and then finish with the mozzarella, basil and Pecorino.

Cook the pizza on top of the stove for about 3 minutes, then transfer the pan to the grill for a further 3–4 minutes.

Serve whole or in slices.

For the tray method
Follow the recipe instructions on page 19. The whole process will take about 90 minutes. Heat the oven to 260°C/gas mark 8 and stretch the dough to the edges of the tray. Be sure to spread your sauce right to the edges before adding toppings. The tray pizza dough serves 4, so quadruple the ingredient quantities. Bake for no less than 10 minutes.

INGREDIENT NOTE

The lamb mince here and the recipe for spicy lamb (see page 60) can both also be used for the meatball pizza (see page 46). Either prepare in advance or after you have shaped the balls, while the dough is rising.

Many people believe the Marinara is a seafood pizza – it is not, but rather a simple vegan pizza that includes no meat or cheese. The name refers to a sailor's wife, *La Marinara*, who might be expected to offer her returning husband something simple and unfussy to eat.

MARINARA BAKED

ingredients, per pizza

1 dough ball (see page 16),
   left to rise for
   1½ –2 hours
flour, for dusting

2 dessertspoons olive oil
1 garlic clove, peeled and
   roughly chopped
4 dessertspoons tomato
   sauce (see page 20)
½ teaspoon dried oregano
4 basil leaves, torn
sea salt and freshly ground
   black pepper

Place a rack on the highest shelf of an oven and turn the grill to its highest setting. When hot, place a greased 26cm iron pan on the stovetop, set to medium heat.

In a saucepan, heat half the olive oil on a low heat and fry the garlic until lightly golden. Stir in the tomato sauce and set aside.

Sprinkle a little flour over your hands and on the work surface and open the dough ball by flattening and stretching the dough with your fingers, or by rolling the dough with a rolling pin. Pick the pizza base up and gently stretch it a little further over your fists without tearing it. Drop this onto the hot pan, and allow it to start rising.

As soon as the dough firms, spread the tomato and garlic sauce over the base with the back of a metal spoon. Drizzle over the remaining olive oil and finish with the oregano.

Cook the pizza on top of the stove for about 3 minutes, then transfer the pan to the grill for a further 3–4 minutes.

Once ready, garnish with fresh basil, season to taste and serve in one piece or sliced.

Cooked ham and mushrooms make a very popular pizza topping, probably because both are fairly moist, with gentle flavours and textures. Good ricotta can also be described in these terms, which is why it is used here to complete the ingredient trilogy.

HAM, MUSHROOM & RICOTTA BAKED

ingredients, per pizza

1 dough ball (see page 16),
 left to rise for
 1½ -2 hours
flour, for dusting

for the *crema di ricotta*
 (makes enough
 for 1 baked pizza)
2 teaspoons milk
4 dessertspoons ricotta
sea salt and freshly ground
 black pepper

for the wild mushrooms
 (makes enough
 for 4 baked pizzas)
160g wild mushrooms
2 dessertspoons extra
 virgin olive oil
pinch of sea salt
2 dessertspoons butter

4 dessertspoons tomato
 sauce (see page 20)
50g cooked York ham,
 cut into small but not
 paper-thin slices
60g *mozzarella fior di
 latte*, torn into 5 chunks
4 basil leaves

Place a rack on the highest shelf of an oven and turn the grill to its highest setting. When hot, place a greased 26cm iron pan on the stovetop, set to medium heat.

Make the crema di ricotta: In a bowl, stir the milk into the ricotta and mix to a smooth consistency. Season with salt and pepper to taste.

Prepare the mushrooms: Rub the wild mushrooms lightly with a tea towel to clean. Do not wash or soak in water. Place in a bowl and toss with the olive oil and salt before frying off in the butter.

Sprinkle a little flour over your hands and on the work surface and open the dough ball by flattening and stretching the dough with your fingers, or by rolling the dough with a rolling pin. Pick the pizza base up and gently stretch it a little further over your fists without tearing it. Drop this onto the hot pan, and allow it to start rising.

As soon as the dough firms up, spread the tomato sauce over the base with the back of a metal spoon and, with a teaspoon, add blobs of *crema di ricotta* (do not spread). Scatter over the ham, basil, mushrooms and mozzarella and drizzle with a little extra olive oil.

Cook the pizza on top of the stove for about 3 minutes, then transfer the pan to the grill for a further 3–4 minutes.

Serve whole or sliced.

INGREDIENT NOTE:
- - - - - - - - - - - - - - - -
A York ham is the quintessential English ham (folklore has it that the oak construction for York Minster provided the sawdust for smoking the ham). It is mild-flavoured and usually lightly smoked. See the method on page 57 for brining your own ham.

If you do not make your own sausage (see page 56) and have no time to prepare lamb mince (see pages 37 or 60) or Italian meatballs (see page 46), choose the chunkiest butcher's sausage you can find. To prepare the sausage, we recommend removing the skin once cooked as it enables you to distribute the meat evenly. Combined with humble mushrooms and the hard bite of a little very mature cheese, this pizza has exceptional flavour.

SAUSAGE WITH FIELD MUSHROOMS & PECORINO   BAKED OR TRAY

ingredients, per pizza

1 dough ball (see page 16),
   left to rise for
   1¹/₂ –2 hours OR
   dough 2 for tray pizzas
flour, for dusting

40g field mushrooms
3 tablespoons extra virgin
   olive oil
pinch of sea salt
1 sausage
4 tablespoons tomato
   sauce (see page 20)
4 basil leaves, shredded
65g *mozzarella fior di
   latte*, torn into 5 chunks
4 teaspoons grated
   Pecorino

Place a rack on the highest shelf of an oven and turn the grill to its highest setting. When hot, place a greased 26cm iron pan on the stovetop, set to medium heat.

Prepare the mushrooms: Clean the field mushrooms by rubbing lightly with a tea towel. Do not wash or soak in water. Place in a bowl and toss with 1 tablespoon olive oil and a little salt. Field mushrooms do not need to be precooked.

Prepare the sausage: Heat 1 tablespoon oil (or lard) with a little water in a heavy pan. As the water reaches the boil, add the sausage and cook, covered, for 15 minutes, then remove the lid and allow the water to evaporate. Wait for the sausage to cool, then remove the skin.

Sprinkle a little flour over your hands and on the work surface and open the dough ball by flattening and stretching the dough with your fingers, or by rolling the dough with a rolling pin. Pick the pizza base up and gently stretch it a little further over your fists without tearing it. Drop this onto the hot pan, and allow it to start rising.

As soon as the dough firms up, spread the tomato sauce over the base with the back of a metal spoon. Drizzle with 1 tablespoon olive oil, crumble over the meat and add the mushrooms, basil and mozzarella, reserving half the Pecorino.

Cook the pizza on top of the stove for about 3 minutes, then transfer the pan to the grill for a further 3–4 minutes.

Sprinkle over the remaining Pecorino and serve whole or in slices.

For the tray method
Follow the recipe instructions on page 19. The whole process will take about 90 minutes. Heat the oven to 260°C/gas mark 8 and stretch the dough to the edges of the tray. Be sure to spread your sauce right to the edges before adding toppings. The tray pizza dough serves 4, so quadruple the ingredient quantities. Bake for no less than 10 minutes.

Wild broccoli, or *friarielli*, tastes like a hybrid of a herb, crossed with a vegetable – a delicious peppery flavour with plenty of scent. It has an 'edge' which is compelling, as do olives, as does smoked cheese. Say no more.

BROCCOLI, OLIVE & SMOKED MOZZARELLA   BAKED

ingredients, per pizza

1 dough ball (see page 16),
   left to rise for
   1½–2 hours
flour, for dusting

for the *friarielli*
   (makes enough
   for 4 baked pizzas)
1 tablespoon extra virgin
   olive oil
1 garlic clove, crushed
½ red chilli, finely
   chopped
200g *friarielli*/wild
   broccoli
sea salt

4 dessertspoons tomato
   sauce (see page 20)
4 kalamata olives
4 basil leaves, torn
60g *mozzarella fior di
   latte*, torn into 5 chunks
20g smoked mozzarella,
   torn into 4 chunks
olive oil, for drizzling

Prepare the friarielli: Heat the oil in a heavy sauté pan and fry the garlic and chilli over a medium heat. Add the leaves, some salt and a drop of water and cover. Cook for about 4 minutes. Drain well and squeeze excess water from the leaves before using.

Place a rack on the highest shelf of an oven and turn the grill to its highest setting. When hot, place a greased 26cm iron pan on the stovetop, set to medium heat.

Sprinkle a little flour over your hands and on the work surface and open the dough ball by flattening and stretching the dough with your fingers, or by rolling the dough with a rolling pin. Pick the pizza base up and gently stretch it a little further over your fists without tearing it. Drop this onto the hot pan, and allow it to start rising.

As soon as the dough firms up, spread the tomato sauce over the base with the back of a metal spoon. Lay some *friarielli* leaves down on the pizza and then top with the olives, basil and both cheeses.

Cook the pizza on top of the stove for about 3 minutes, then transfer the pan to the grill for a further 3–4 minutes.

Once ready, drizzle with a little olive oil to finish.

INGREDIENT NOTE
- - - - - - - - - - - - - - - -
Smoked mozzarella adds a wonderful dimension to certain pizzas and can also be used in salads. If you wish to smoke your own cheese, follow the recipe on page 23.

This is a family pizza with much rolling of meatballs required, which means kids, if you have them, can get involved. Make the balls small and plentiful – the more the merrier, in every respect!

ITALIAN MEATBALLS BAKED OR TRAY

ingredients, per pizza

1 dough ball (see page 16),
   left to rise for
   1¹/₂ –2 hours OR
   dough 2 for tray pizzas
flour, for dusting

**for the Italian meatballs
   (makes enough
   for 4 baked pizzas)**
1 slice bread (no crust)
1 egg yolk
200g reduced tomato
   sauce (see page 20)
1 garlic clove, crushed
100g veal mince
100g beef mince
50g mortadella
30g Parmesan, grated
sea salt and freshly ground
   black pepper
1 tablespoon chopped
   flat-leaf parsley

80g *mozzarella fior di
   latte*, torn into 6 chunks
4 basil leaves, torn
several shavings Parmesan
1 teaspoon chopped
   parsley
chilli oil, optional
   (see page 80)

Make the meatballs: Soak the bread in the egg yolk and mash it with a fork. In a large bowl, mix all the meatball ingredients together and roll into small balls.

In a large pan, heat the tomato sauce and, when simmering, drop the meatballs in and cook for about 8 minutes.

Place a rack on the highest shelf of an oven and turn the grill to its highest setting. When hot, place a greased 26cm iron pan on the stovetop, set to medium heat.

Sprinkle a little flour over your hands and on the work surface and open the dough ball by flattening and stretching the dough with your fingers, or by rolling the dough with a rolling pin. Pick the pizza base up and gently stretch it a little further over your fists without tearing it. Drop this onto the hot pan, and allow it to start rising.

As soon as the dough firms up, spread 5 meatballs with their sauce around the pizza and add the mozzarella and basil.

Cook the pizza on top of the stove for about 3 minutes, then transfer the pan to the grill for a further 3–4 minutes.

Once ready, finish off with the Parmesan shavings and freshly chopped parsley. Serve with chilli oil on the side.

For the tray method
Follow the recipe instructions on page 19. The whole process will take about 90 minutes. Heat the oven to 260˚C/gas mark 8 and stretch the dough to the edges of the tray. Be sure to spread your sauce right to the edges before adding toppings. The tray pizza dough serves 4, so quadruple the ingredient quantities. Bake for no less than 10 minutes.

INGREDIENT NOTE

Classic Italian meatballs contain a mixture of veal, pork and beef. Chuck is a good cut of beef for mincing.
   If you cannot find mortadella, use half minced shoulder of pork and half streaky bacon.

MIXED LEAF SALAD

FOGLIA DI
INSALATA MISTA

This is Franco Manca's house salad recipe. Alfalfa sprouts have a lovely peppery quality and if you have fresh, ripe avocado or fennel, both make great additional ingredients.

SERVES 4
32 cherry tomatoes, quartered
100g cucumber, sliced and quartered
40g alfalfa sprouts
600g mixed leaves
a good sprig of mint leaves

MUSTARD AND HONEY VINAIGRETTE (MAKES 500ML)
125ml cider vinegar
1 teaspoon yellow mustard seeds
1 teaspoon black mustard seeds
1 dessertspoon organic mustard
1 dessertspoon clear honey
1 teaspoon dried oregano
175ml rapeseed oil
125ml extra virgin olive oil
sea salt and freshly ground black pepper, to taste

Simply wash, prep and toss together the salad ingredients.

To make the vinaigrette: Use a blender, food processor, a small balloon whisk or handheld electric blitzer to combine all the ingredients. Whatever you do, always start with the vinegar and other ingredients and add the oil in stages. This will make a more successful emulsion. The mustard (a protein) in the recipe helps to stabilise the emulsion so that it does not easily separate.

ROCKET & PARMESAN SALAD

RUCOLA E
PARMIGIANO
INSALATA

A simple watercress or rocket salad works well with pizzas, dressed with shavings of Parmesan and a little balsamic vinegar.

SERVES 4
640g rocket
320g Parmesan, shaved into curls
1 tablespoon balsamic vinegar
2 tablespoons extra virgin olive oil
sea salt and freshly ground black pepper

Combine all the ingredients in a large bowl and toss to mix. Season to taste.

This is a fairly hot, spicy pizza, though the heat is nicely balanced by the salty bacon. Sweet chillis are not actually that sweet, just more so than red chillis. Try and find the best quality bacon you can find and make sure it is sliced thinly.

BACON, SWEET GREEN CHILLI
& ROCKET BAKED

ingredients, per pizza

1 dough ball (see page 16),
   left to rise for
   1¹/₂ –2 hours
flour, for dusting

1 sweet green chilli
4 dessertspoons tomato
   sauce (see page 20)
1 dessertspoon extra virgin
   olive oil (or lard)
3 slices streaky bacon
4 basil leaves, torn
60g *mozzarella fior di
   latte*, torn into 5 chunks
a handful of rocket
   (optional)

Place a rack on the highest shelf of an oven and turn the grill to its highest setting. When hot, place a greased 26cm iron pan on the stovetop, set to medium heat.

Prepare the chilli: Heat the chilli over a gas ring on the naked flame, or on a hot barbecue so that the skin burns. Keep turning until the chilli is scorched and the skin starts to blister. Set aside to cool, then slice in half and scrape out the seeds.

Sprinkle a little flour over your hands and on the work surface and open the dough ball by flattening and stretching the dough with your fingers, or by rolling the dough with a rolling pin. Pick the pizza base up and gently stretch it a little further over your fists without tearing it. Drop this onto the hot pan, and allow it to start rising.

As soon as the dough firms up, spread the tomato sauce over the base using the back of a metal spoon. Drizzle with olive oil (or lard), then arrange the bacon, chilli, basil and mozzarella on top.

Cook the pizza on top of the stove for about 3 minutes, then transfer the pan to the grill for a further 3–4 minutes.

Once ready, dress with rocket, if you like, and serve whole or in slices.

INGREDIENT NOTE

Although the saltiness of the bacon provides balance in this recipe, it can sometimes overpower. To temper it a little, poach it in off-the-boil water for 5 minutes before using.

The best peppers usually start in July and end in September. Yellow peppers are the sweetest and you can make this pizza with yellow peppers only, if you wish. There is no mozzarella on this pizza as the freshness of the peppers is compromised by cooked cheese. Do not be tempted to adjust this – when you try it, you'll taste why.

SCORCHED RED & YELLOW
PEPPERS BAKED

ingredients, per pizza

1 dough ball (see page 16),
　　left to rise for
　　1 1/2 –2 hours
flour, for dusting

for the salsa

100g fresh tomatoes
1/2 teaspoon salt
1/2 garlic clove, crushed
1/2 tablespoon finely
　　chopped onion
2 basil leaves, chopped

for the peppers
　　(makes enough
　　for 4 baked pizzas)

2 yellow peppers
1 red pepper
1/2 garlic clove, crushed
flat-leaf parsley, chopped,
　　to taste
2 tablespoons olive oil
sea salt and freshly ground
　　black pepper

Prepare the salsa: Place the tomatoes in a bowl and cover with boiling water. Leave for about 3 minutes, then remove and allow to cool slightly. Peel, de-seed and chop the tomatoes. Transfer to a sieve, sprinkle with salt and let the tomatoes drain for about 20 minutes. In a bowl, mix the tomatoes with the garlic, onion and basil.

Prepare the peppers: Heat each pepper over a gas ring on the naked flame, or on a hot barbecue, so that the skin burns. Keep turning until the skin is black. Set aside to cool before scraping the skin away with the back of a small knife. Cut the peppers open, spoon out the seeds and cut into long strips. Transfer to a small bowl and combine with the garlic, parsley, olive oil and a grind of pepper and a pinch of salt. Leave to marinate for 1 hour.

Place a rack on the highest shelf of an oven and turn the grill to its highest setting. When hot, place a greased 26cm iron pan on the stovetop, set to medium heat.

Sprinkle a little flour over your hands and on the work surface and open the dough ball by flattening and stretching the dough with your fingers, or by rolling the dough with a rolling pin. Pick the pizza base up and gently stretch it a little further over your fists without tearing it. Drop this onto the hot pan, and allow it to start rising.

As soon as the dough firms up, turn the heat down to medium and spread the tomato salsa over the base with the back of a metal spoon. Drizzle with a little extra oil.

Cook the pizza on top of the stove for about 3 minutes, then transfer the pan to the grill for a further 3–4 minutes.

Once ready, add the peppers and serve in one piece or sliced.

The *Treviggiana* is a sort of radicchio that, in its *tardivo* form, looks a little like a tentacled octopus. It has more latent sweetness than other varieties, which comes through as it roasts off and caramelises. In Treviso, a region to the North of Venice, where this radicchio is grown, we have even been served radicchio ice cream! It is seasonal but available through several food importers.

RADICCHIO, REGGIANA & STILTON BAKED

ingredients, per pizza

1 dough ball (see page 16), left to rise for 1¹/₂ –2 hours
flour, for dusting

for the radicchio (makes enough for 4 baked pizzas)
120g (16 leaves) radicchio leaves, washed
2 tablespoons olive oil
generous pinch of salt

1 dessertspoon extra virgin olive oil
60g *mozzarella fior di latte*, torn into 5 chunks
65g blue cheese, crumbled into 5 chunks
4 teaspoons grated Parmesan
garlic oil (optional)

Prepare the radicchio: In a large bowl, mix the radicchio with the olive oil and salt and leave to marinate for 40 minutes.

Place a rack on the highest shelf of an oven and turn the grill to its highest setting. When hot, place a greased 26cm iron pan on the stovetop, set to medium heat.

Sprinkle a little flour over your hands and on the work surface and open the dough ball by flattening and stretching the dough with your fingers, or by rolling the dough with a rolling pin. Pick the pizza base up and gently stretch it a little further over your fists without tearing it. Drop this onto the hot pan, and allow it to start rising.

As soon as the dough firms up, drizzle with the olive oil and add the mozzarella and marinated radicchio leaves. Top with the blue cheese and half the grated Parmesan.

Cook the pizza on top of the stove for about 3 minutes, then transfer the pan to the grill for a further 3–4 minutes.

Dress with the remaining Parmesan and serve in pieces or whole, with an extra drizzle of garlic oil if you have it.

In Naples and the surrounding area, this combination of a juicy, thick-cut pork sausage and wild broccoli is an autumn-winter classic. Both are favoured farm ingredients and at their very best at this time of year. However, as wild broccoli can be a little hard to find, *cime di rape* (turnip tops) are often substituted and make a very good alternative.

SAUSAGE WITH WILD BROCCOLI BAKED

ingredients, per pizza

1 dough ball (see page 16),
    left to rise for
    1½–2 hours
flour, for dusting

for the *friarielli*
    (makes enough
    for 4 baked pizzas)
2 teaspoons extra virgin
    olive oil
1 garlic clove, crushed
½ red chilli, finely
    chopped
200g *friarielli*/wild
    broccoli

1 sausage (see page 56)
75g *mozzarella fior di
    latte*, torn into
    6–8 chunks
1½ tablespoons extra
    virgin olive oil
5 slices Gruyère
5 teaspoons grated
    Pecorino
2 teaspoons truffle oil
    (optional)

Prepare the friarielli: Heat the oil in a heavy sauté pan and fry the garlic and chilli over a medium heat. Add the leaves, some salt and a drop of water and cover. Cook for about 4 minutes. Drain well and squeeze excess water from the leaves before using.

Prepare the sausage: Set a heavy sauté pan, with enough water to coat the bottom and 1 tablespoon olive oil (or lard), on the stove over a medium heat. As the water comes to the boil, add the sausage and cook, covered, for about 15 minutes, then take the lid off and allow the water to evaporate. Let the sausage cool, then remove the skin.

Place a rack on the highest shelf of an oven and turn the grill to its highest setting. When hot, place a greased 26cm iron pan on the stovetop, set to medium heat.

Sprinkle a little flour over your hands and on the work surface and open the dough ball by flattening and stretching the dough with your fingers, or by rolling the dough with a rolling pin. Pick the pizza base up and gently stretch it a little further over your fists without tearing it. Drop this onto the hot pan, and allow it to start rising.

As soon as the dough firms up, distribute the *friarielli* over the base and add the sausage, mozzarella, Gruyère and a drizzle of olive oil.

Cook the pizza on top of the stove for about 3 minutes, then transfer the pan to the grill for a further 3–4 minutes.

Once ready, sprinkle the Pecorino over the pizza, drizzle with the truffle oil, if using, and serve whole or in slices.

MAKING YOUR OWN SAUSAGE

Making your own sausage is not difficult at all and can be a lot of fun. If you have a sausage-making machine, by all means use that, but it's not necessary at all – you just need good meat, simple flavourings, some natural hog casing (which you can source online or ask for at your local butcher's) and the aid of a wooden spoon or ladle handle.

Hog casings are stored in salt so should be washed before use to soften them up. Soak them in water, mixed with a little vinegar, for 1 hour (or overnight).

This sausage recipe can also be used as a delicious mince topping. If you would like to make it extra spicy, add 30g chilli paste (see page 80) into the mix.

MAKES APPROX 10 SAUSAGES

approx. 2 metres hog casing, washed and soaked
1kg pork (equal parts belly, shoulder and neck),
  cold out of the fridge
20g salt
5–10g freshly ground black pepper
10g fennel seeds
50ml white wine or cider

With a very sharp knife, cut the pork into small pieces (about 5g each). Using a knife is best but, if you have a meat mincer, you can also use this on its coarsest setting.

In a large stainless-steel, plastic or glass bowl, mix all the ingredients together until thoroughly combined and rest in a sealed container in the fridge for 3 days, for the flavours to meld.

With the help of a funnel and the aid of a wooden spoon or ladle handle, gently stuff the sausage meat into the hog casing, taking great care that the skin does not tear.

After you have filled the casing, twist the sausages a few times at the lengths you desire.

Hang in a cold place (10°C) like a garland, so the sausages are kept apart and air can circulate around them. Leave them for a day, to give them extra flavour.

Hygiene note
Keep your hands, work surface and equipment (especially knives) all super clean and work with cold meat fresh from the fridge.

BRINING YOUR OWN HAM

As well as providing a great pizza topping, this ham will serve multiple purposes – delicious in sandwiches, salads, you name it. This recipe contains no extra spices or flavours as it rests on using a really good-quality, free-range farm animal. The best kind is from a free-roaming pig on a diet of just chestnuts and acorns and this is why the best pork comes at the end of autumn or the beginning of winter. The fat they have accumulated to get them through the cold months has an incredible taste and is almost the best part of the animal.

A shoulder of ham is often very large and so you can also use a shoulder of pork that is similar and also very tasty. Make sure that the shoulder bone (scapula) is removed as otherwise it will inhibit the brining.

boned shoulder of ham
70g salt
5g sugar per litre of water

Place the ham in a large saucepan, cover with water and bring to the boil. Add the salt and 5g sugar per litre of water, then take off the heat and allow to cool. Cover the container and set aside in the fridge or a cold garage for 8 days.

Discard the brine and give the ham a quick rinse under cold running water. Clean out the container, then place the brined shoulder back in the pot and cover with water. Place on the heat and bring to a simmer, add the salt and sugar again like before and leave to cook for 20–25 minutes per kg of meat. Try to keep the water just off the boil if you can.

Remove the ham from the brine and pat dry with kitchen paper, then place on a wire rack to cool completely.

If you would like a caramelised finish, roast the ham briefly with a glaze of molasses, or simply store as it is.

You can use homemade sausage in the following recipes:

Sausage with Field Mushrooms & Pecorino p. 43
Sausage with Wild Broccoli p. 55
Pork Sausage with Roasted Peppers & Parmesan p. 58

You can use home-brined ham in the following recipe:

Ham, Mushrooms & Ricotta p. 42

The mix of garlic, capers, basil and roasted peppers in this recipe acts like a single ingredient to counterbalance the meatiness of the sausage. Pork sausage works best, as it is lighter in flavour than beef, though lamb can also be used.

PORK SAUSAGE, ROASTED PEPPERS & PARMESAN BAKED OR TRAY

ingredients, per pizza

1 dough ball (see page 16),
  left to rise for
  1½–2 hours OR
  dough 2 for tray pizzas
flour, for dusting

**for the peppers with
  capers and garlic
  (makes enough
  for 4 pizzas)**
2 garlic cloves, crushed
½ teaspoon salt
5 basil leaves, torn
4 capers
200g roasted red peppers,
  cut into long strips
  (see page 52)

1 sausage (see page 56)
1 dessertspoon olive oil
4 teaspoons grated
  Parmesan
4 basil leaves, torn
a handful of rocket
  (optional)

Make the roasted peppers: In a large bowl, mix all the ingredients together and leave to marinate for 1 hour before using.

Prepare the sausage: Set a heavy sauté pan, with enough water to coat the bottom and 1 tablespoon olive oil (or lard), on the stove over a medium heat. As the water comes to the boil, add the sausage and cook, covered, for about 15 minutes, then take the lid off and allow the water to evaporate. Let the sausage cool, then remove the skin.

Place a rack on the highest shelf of an oven and turn the grill to its highest setting. When hot, place a greased 26cm iron pan on the stovetop, set to medium heat.

Sprinkle a little flour over your hands and on the work surface and open the dough ball by flattening and stretching the dough with your fingers, or by rolling the dough with a rolling pin. Pick the pizza base up and gently stretch it a little further over your fists without tearing it. Drop this onto the hot pan, and allow it to start rising.

As soon as the dough firms up, turn the heat down to medium and drizzle the base with olive oil. Add a quarter of the roasted pepper mix, the Parmesan, basil and cooked sausage.

Cook the pizza on top of the stove for about 3 minutes, then transfer the pan to the grill for a further 3–4 minutes.

Once this is ready, scatter with rocket, if using, and serve in one piece or sliced.

For the tray method
Follow the recipe instructions on page 19. The whole process will take about 90 minutes. Heat the oven to 260°C/gas mark 8 and stretch the dough to the edges of the tray. Be sure to spread your sauce right to the edges before adding toppings. The tray pizza dough serves 4, so quadruple the ingredient quantities. Bake for no less than 10 minutes.

If you want to get hot without getting too heavy, this is the pizza for you. Make your lamb mix as spicy as you dare and balance with tangy tomato sauce (reduced if you prefer a more punchy flavour) and your molten mozzarella.

SPICY LAMB, MOZZARELLA
& TOMATO BAKED OR TRAY

ingredients, per pizza

1 dough ball (see page 16),
   left to rise for
   1½ –2 hours OR
   dough 2 for tray pizzas
flour, for dusting

for the spicy lamb
(makes enough
for 4 baked pizzas)
1 tablespoon olive oil
4 garlic cloves, 3 roasted,
   1 finely chopped
²/₃ scotch bonnet chilli,
   deseeded and chopped
a pinch of paprika
300g lamb (or lamb
   mince)

1 dessertspoon extra virgin
   olive oil
4 dessertspoons tomato
   sauce (see page 20)
4 basil leaves, torn
65g *mozzarella fior di
   latte*, torn into 6 chunks
4 teaspoons grated
   Pecorino
1 teaspoon garlic oil
   (optional)

Make the spicy lamb mince: Heat the oil in a heavy sauté pan and fry the garlic and chilli slowly over a low heat until the garlic browns. Remove from the heat and add the paprika. Remove the skin from the roasted garlic, then place everything in a large bowl with the meat and mince together. (If using already-minced meat, combine thoroughly.) Leave to marinate before using.

Place a rack on the highest shelf of an oven and turn the grill to its highest setting. When hot, place a greased 26cm iron pan on the stovetop, set to medium heat.

Sprinkle a little flour over your hands and on the work surface and open the dough ball by flattening and stretching the dough with your fingers, or by rolling the dough with a rolling pin. Pick the pizza base up and gently stretch it a little further over your fists without tearing it. Drop this onto the hot pan, and allow it to start rising.

As soon as the dough firms up, spread the tomato sauce over the base with the back of a spoon. Distribute a quarter of the lamb mince over the top and add the rest of the ingredients, reserving some Pecorino to finish.

Cook the pizza on top of the stove for about 3 minutes, then transfer the pan to the grill for a further 3–4 minutes.

Once ready, sprinkle with the remaining Pecorino, drizzle with garlic oil, if using, and serve in one piece or sliced.

For the tray method
Follow the recipe instructions on page 19. The whole process will take about 90 minutes. Heat the oven to 260°C/gas mark 8 and stretch the dough to the edges of the tray. Be sure to spread your sauce right to the edges before adding toppings. The tray pizza dough serves 4, so quadruple the ingredient quantities. Bake for no less than 10 minutes.

Caramelised onion with pancetta or bacon is a great pairing but we also love the vegetarian combination of blue cheese and spinach. For blue cheese we use Stilton and a fairly firm goat's cheese. The spinach is simply seared with a little garlic oil.

SPINACH, CARAMELISED ONION, GOAT'S CHEESE & STILTON   BAKED

ingredients, per pizza

1 dough ball (see page 16), left to rise for 1½–2 hours
flour, for dusting

for the caramelised onion
(makes enough
for 4 baked pizzas)

1 large onion, thinly sliced in rings
1 dessertspoon olive oil
1 teaspoon cane sugar
½ teaspoon vinegar

for the spinach
(makes enough
for 4 baked pizzas)

1 dessertspoon extra virgin olive oil
½ red chilli, finely chopped (optional)
1 garlic clove, crushed
260g spinach
pinch of sea salt

1 dessertspoon olive oil
20g blue cheese
20g goat's cheese
60g *mozzarella fior di latte*, torn into 5 chunks

Make the caramelised onion: Heat the oil in a frying pan and sweat the onion over a low heat for about 20 minutes. Add a bit of water if they start to stick. (If the onions burn, discard them.) When they have turned a golden colour, stir in the sugar and vinegar and reduce the temperature further. After about 15 minutes, the onions should have caramelised.

Prepare the spinach: Heat the oil in a heavy sauté pan and fry the chilli and garlic. Add the leaves, salt and a drop of water and cover. Cook for about 4 minutes. Drain well and squeeze excess water from the leaves before using.

Place a rack on the highest shelf of an oven and turn the grill to its highest setting. When hot, place a greased 26cm iron pan on the stovetop, set to medium heat.

Sprinkle a little flour over your hands and on the work surface and open the dough ball by flattening and stretching the dough with your fingers, or by rolling the dough with a rolling pin. Pick the pizza base up and gently stretch it a little further over your fists without tearing it. Drop this onto the hot pan, and allow it to start rising.

As soon as the dough firms up, drizzle with the olive oil and distribute a quarter of the caramelised onion and spinach over the base and top with the blue cheese, goat's cheese and mozzarella.

Cook the pizza on top of the stove for about 3 minutes, then transfer the pan to the grill for a further 3–4 minutes.

Serve whole or in slices.

Butternut squash is a wonderful ingredient that we prefer to the usual pumpkins available in Italy. It caramelises beautifully in the oven and its sweetness, offset by the blue cheese, makes this pizza work very well. The roasted pine nuts are simply a decadent addition.

STILTON, BUTTERNUT SQUASH & PINE NUTS BAKED

ingredients, per pizza

1 dough ball (see page 16),
   left to rise for
   1½ –2 hours
flour, for dusting

for the butternut squash (makes enough for 4 baked pizzas)

180g butternut squash,
   peeled and cut into
   small wedges
2 tablespoons extra virgin
   olive oil
sea salt

1 dessertspoon pine nuts
1 dessertspoon extra virgin
   olive oil
65g *mozzarella fior di
   latte*, torn into 6 chunks
20g blue cheese (Stilton),
   crumbled into 5 chunks
3 teaspoons basil pesto
   (see page 34)

Prepare the butternut squash: Preheat the oven to 220°C/gas mark 7. Coat the wedges in olive oil, sprinkle with salt and bake in the oven for 40 minutes, turning once. Reduce the heat to 180°C/gas mark 4 after 20 minutes.

Scatter the pine nuts over a baking tray and roast off under the grill, being careful not to let them burn. Set aside.

Place a rack on the highest shelf of the oven and turn the grill up to its highest setting. When hot, place a greased 26cm iron pan on the stovetop, set to medium heat.

Sprinkle a little flour over your hands and on the work surface and open the dough ball by flattening and stretching the dough with your fingers, or by rolling the dough with a rolling pin. Pick the pizza base up and gently stretch it a little further over your fists without tearing it. Drop this onto the hot pan, and allow it to start rising.

As soon as the dough firms up, drizzle with olive oil and distribute the butternut squash over the base. Scatter with the mozzarella and blue cheese.

Cook the pizza on top of the stove for about 3 minutes, then transfer the pan to the grill for a further 3–4 minutes.

Before serving, use a teaspoon to dot the pizza with basil pesto and sprinkle with the toasted pine nuts.

The small, fruity tomatoes cut through the richness of the salami and smoked mozzarella on this pizza, particularly if you roast the cherry tomatoes to enhance their sweetness. Otherwise, the tomatoes can be baked or added fresh at the end.

SALAMI, SMOKED BUFFALO CHEESE & CHERRY TOMATOES BAKED

ingredients, per pizza

1 dough ball (see page 16), left to rise for 1^1/$_2$ –2 hours

flour, for dusting

1 dessertspoon extra virgin olive oil

8 slices salami ('nduja, if possible)

5 cherry tomatoes, halved

50g smoked buffalo mozzarella, torn into 5 chunks

a handful of rocket

a few grinds of black pepper

Place a rack on the highest shelf of an oven and turn the grill to its highest setting. When hot, place a greased 26cm iron pan on the stovetop, set to medium heat.

Sprinkle a little flour over your hands and on the work surface and open the dough ball by flattening and stretching the dough with your fingers, or by rolling the dough with a rolling pin. Pick the pizza base up and gently stretch it a little further over your fists without tearing it. Drop this onto the hot pan, and allow it to start rising.

As soon as the dough firms up, drizzle the olive oil over the base. Lay the salami down on the pizza, then add the cherry tomatoes and mozzarella.

Cook the pizza on top of the stove for about 3 minutes, then transfer the pan to the grill for a further 3–4 minutes.

Once ready, dress with rocket and serve with a grind of black pepper and a little more olive oil.

INGREDIENT NOTE

Use 'nduja if you can, a wonderful spicy Calabrian salami that is so soft it is almost spreadable. The fat melts into the pizza and moistens the base. See the method for making your own on page 69.

Cured pig's cheek, or *guanciale*, is sweeter than pancetta and smells even better than bacon. It is very fatty and rich and, all in all, heavenly (find the method on page 70 for how to make your own). Since melted cheese has a fairly oily texture, you are better off using fresh buffalo cheese in this recipe. The potato, though quite 'dry', doesn't actually absorb excess fat, but certainly benefits from its presence in terms of flavour.

SMOKED MOZZARELLA, BAKED POTATO & PIG'S CHEEK BAKED OR TRAY

ingredients, per pizza

1 dough ball (see page 16),
  left to rise for
  1½ -2 hours OR
  dough 2 for tray pizzas
flour, for dusting

for the potato topping
  (makes enough
  for 4 baked pizzas)
320g Maris Piper potatoes,
  cut into small wedges
3 tablespoons olive oil
1 teaspoon fine sea salt
½ onion, finely sliced
60g cherry tomatoes,
  halved

1 dessertspoon extra virgin
  olive oil (or lard)
40g pig's cheek, thinly
  sliced
60g smoked mozzarella,
  torn into 5 chunks
40g buffalo mozzarella,
  torn into 4 chunks
4 teaspoons grated
  Parmesan

Make the potato topping: Preheat the oven to 200°C/gas mark 4. In a roasting pan, mix the potatoes with 2 tablespoons olive oil and sea salt and bake in the oven for about 40 minutes. Drain on kitchen paper.

Heat 1 tablespoon olive oil in a heavy sauté pan over a low heat and sweat the onion. Turn up the heat slightly and add the cherry tomatoes. When the ingredients caramelise and become sticky, add the potato wedges and turn off the heat.

Place a rack on the highest shelf of an oven and turn the grill to its highest setting. When hot, place a greased 26cm iron pan on the stovetop, set to medium heat.

Sprinkle a little flour over your hands and on the work surface and open the dough ball by flattening and stretching the dough with your fingers, or by rolling the dough with a rolling pin. Pick the pizza base up and gently stretch it a little further over your fists without tearing it. Drop this onto the hot pan, and allow it to start rising.

As soon as the dough firms up, turn the heat down to medium and drizzle the olive oil or lard over the base. Arrange the pig's cheek, mozzarella and a quarter of the potatoes on top and sprinkle with half the Parmesan.

Cook the pizza on top of the stove for about 3 minutes, then transfer the pan to the grill for a further 3–4 minutes.

Once ready, finish with a few clumps of fresh buffalo mozzarella and sprinkle with the remaining Parmesan.

For the tray method
Follow the recipe instructions on page 19. The whole process will take about 90 minutes. Heat the oven to 260°C/gas mark 8 and stretch the dough to the edges of the tray. Be sure to spread your sauce right to the edges before adding toppings. The tray pizza dough serves 4, so quadruple the ingredient quantities. Bake for no less than 10 minutes.

CURING

It is well worth curing at home, as all you need is good-quality meat, curing salts and the right ambient environment – either a cellar with a temperature of 10–12˚C and a good level of humidity (about 85%), or a fermentation cell. Unless you have the latter, curing should take place during the cooler months of the year.

Curing salts
The dry climate of southern Italy creates the perfect curing environment, where bad bacteria rarely thrive, and so our recipes simply use coarse sea salt rather than curing salts. However, sadly, it is difficult to recreate such a climate at home and so, to be on the safe side, it is advisable to use curing salts, which will protect against botulism.

SALAMI

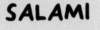

SALSICCIA SECCA

This basic salami cures in just 2 weeks. It has no time to develop the classic exterior mould but it is very tasty and easy to make.

MAKES ABOUT 3–4 THIN SALAMI
**1kg pork (equal parts belly, shoulder and neck),
  cold out of the fridge
26g salt (or curing salts)
7ml vinegar
5–10g freshly ground black pepper
5g fennel seeds, optional
60cm hog casing, washed and soaked
butcher's string, for tying**

Variation
You can make a spicy version by adding about 20g of the chilli paste from page 80.

With a very sharp knife, cut the pork into small pieces (about 5g each). Using a knife is best but if you have a meat mincer you can use this on its coarsest setting.

In a large stainless-steel, plastic or glass bowl, mix all the ingredients together until thoroughly combined. With the help of a funnel and a wooden spoon handle, gently stuff the meat into the casing, filling to approx. 25cm and then tying off with butcher's string. Pack the meat tightly so no air gets trapped and prick the sausage all over to release any air that is left.

Hang the salami in a warm, humid environment for 12 hours. This is what we call *stufatura*, which starts the fermentation process. One way to do this is to hang the salami over a pan of simmering water on the stove, or to place a large bowl of hot water under the hanging meat(refresh the hot water 3–4 times over 12 hours).

Transfer the salami to a cellar or fermentation cell with a temperature of 10–12˚C and a humidity level of about 85%. After 2 weeks your salami will be ready.

SPICY CALABRIAN SALAMI

'NDUJA

This is a very soft, fatty, almost spreadable salami that works wonders on pizza. The spiciness will depend on the strength of the chilli. You might use anything from hot scotch bonnets to very mild ancho chillies. The latter can be slightly roasted before use, which will add good extra flavour.

MAKES ABOUT 3–4 THIN SALAMI

1kg pork (400g shoulder, 500g cheek and 100g back fat)
23g salt (or curing salts)
80g dried red chilli
10g chilli powder (or pimienton or Hungarian paprika)
1 metre hog casing, washed and soaked
butcher's string, for tying

In a mincer, chop the meat to a very fine mince. If you do not have one, use a sharp butcher's knife and work until you have a very fine grain.

In a large stainless-steel, plastic or glass bowl, mix all the ingredients together until thoroughly combined. With the help of a funnel and a wooden spoon handle, gently stuff the meat into the casing, filling to approx. 25cm and then tying off with butcher's string. Pack the meat tightly so no air gets trapped and prick the sausage all over to release any air that is left.

Hang the 'nduja in a warm, humid environment for 12 hours. One way to do this is to hang the salami over a pan of simmering water on the stove or to place a large bowl of hot water under the hanging meat. Refresh the hot water 3–4 times over 12 hours.

Transfer the 'nduja to a cellar or fermentation cell with a temperature of 10–12˚C and a humidity level of about 85%. After 3–4 weeks it will be ready.

Preserving salami
One very effective way of preserving salami is to cut it into small pieces and pack into a sterilised, sealable jam jar. Pack in as much salami as possible. Gently melt some lard (or other animal fat), without allowing it to fry, and pour into the jar until it reaches the top. Seal and store in a cool, dark place for up to 6 months. Once opened, keep sealed in the fridge and add a teaspoon to a pizza, or when making sauces, to add flavour.

PIG'S CHEEK

GUANCIALE

This is similar to bacon but the meat is taken from the cheek bone. It is fattier than bacon and has a sweet finish that works very well on pizza. You can substitute this for bacon in any of recipes in this book.

pig's cheek (a triangular shape with thick skin on one side)
coarse salt (to cover), or curing salt
25ml white wine
25ml vinegar
freshly ground black pepper or chilli flakes (to cover)

Roll the meat in the coarse salt and place in a sealed container in the fridge or in a cool place (5–9°C). Rotate every day for 6 days.

After 6 days, mix the wine and vinegar together in a bowl. Scrub the salt off the meat and lightly wash the flesh side in the wine-vinegar mixture. Pat dry with kitchen paper.

Make a hole in one end of the meat and pass a kitchen rod through it for hanging. Cover the flesh and the hole in either ground black pepper or chilli flakes, or wrap in a cloth to keep flies away.

Hang in a cellar or fermentation cell with a temperature of 10–12°C and a humidity level of about 85%. After 5 weeks your *guanciale* will be ready.

When cooking, remove the chilli or pepper coating from the meat.

ITALIAN AIR-CURED BEEF

BRESAOLA

The best meat to use for bresaola is that from a large steer. The cut is usually referred to as a 'round roast', or *magatello* in Italian. However, you can also use a rolled haunch of venison.

You can easily source bungs (large, natural meat casings) on the internet. Like hog casings, ox bungs must be washed in a water and vinegar solution before use.

Bresaola makes a very good antipasto on its own, with pepper, oil and lemon. Slice as thinly as possible.

85g coarse sea salt
10g freshly ground black pepper
2g sugar
2kg round roast beef
1 ox bung
butcher's string

In a container, mix the salt, pepper and sugar together and roll the beef in this mixture, coating thoroughly. Refrigerate, turning and massaging the meat every day for 9 days (larger cuts will need longer).

After 9 days, push the meat into the ox bung and tie off the ends tightly with butcher's string. Hang in a warm environment (20°C) with an ideal humidity of 70% for 2 days. To ensure it is not too dry, place a bowl of hot water under the beef so the rising humidity can reach it. Repeat this once a day.

After 2 days, move the bresaola to a cellar or curing chamber with a temperature of 12–15°C for 28 days. Once the meat has lost one-third of its weight, it is ready to taste. Either vacuum-pack or wrap in foil, and use within a few weeks.

CURED LARD

LARDO

This is cured back fat and, if you mince it very finely, it will melt quickly on a pizza to delicious effect. Use in small quantities – about 4g per pizza.

500g–2kg pork back fat
coarse sea salt (to cover)
freshly ground black pepper (to cover)

Cover the fat in coarse sea salt and place in a sealed container in the fridge or in a cool place (5–9°C). Rotate every day for 5 (for 500g) to 8 (for 2kg) days.

Cover the fat in pepper and hang in a cellar or fermentation cell with a temperature of 10–12°C and a humidity level of about 80%. After 4 weeks your lardo will be ready.

You can use any mix of wild mushrooms for this pizza, including oyster, chanterelles, porcini etc., depending on what is available (do not be tempted to pick these in the wild unless you know what you are doing). Although not as exotic, field mushrooms can also be used. In the British Isles, look out in springtime for Mousseron mushrooms, which are good and affordable.

WILD MUSHROOM BAKED, TRAY OR FRIED

ingredients, per pizza

1 dough ball (see page 16),
   left to rise for
   1½ –2 hours OR
   dough 2 for tray pizzas
flour, for dusting

**for the wild mushrooms
   (makes enough
   for 4 baked pizzas)**
160g wild mushrooms
2 dessertspoons butter
2 dessertspoons extra
   virgin olive oil
pinch of sea salt

**for the *crema di ricotta*
   (makes enough
   for 1 baked pizzas)**
2 teaspoons milk
4 dessertspoons ricotta
salt and freshly ground
   black pepper

1 dessertspoon extra virgin
   olive oil
60g *mozzarella fior di
   latte*, torn into 5 chunks
garlic-infused olive oil
   (optional)

Prepare the wild mushrooms: Rub the wild mushrooms with a damp tea towel to remove any mulch. Do not soak them in water or they become slimy. Heat the olive oil and butter in a frying pan over a low heat and sear the wild mushrooms for about 3 minutes, seasoning with a pinch of salt. If you are using field mushrooms, simply rub them clean and thinly slice (they do not need to be pre-cooked).

Make the crema di ricotta: In a bowl, stir the milk into the ricotta and mix to a smooth consistency. Season with salt and pepper to taste.

Place a rack on the highest shelf of an oven and turn the grill to its highest setting. When hot, place a greased 26cm iron pan on the stovetop, set to medium heat.

Sprinkle a little flour over your hands and on the work surface and open the dough ball by flattening and stretching the dough with your fingers, or by rolling the dough with a rolling pin. Pick the pizza base up and gently stretch it a little further over your fists without tearing it. Drop this onto the hot pan, and allow it to start rising.

As soon as the base firms up, spread the *crema di ricotta* over the base with the back of a metal spoon. Drizzle with the olive oil and scatter the mushrooms and mozzarella on top.

Cook the pizza on top of the stove for about 3 minutes, then transfer the pan to the grill for a further 3–4 minutes.

Serve in one piece or sliced, with a drizzle of garlic-infused olive oil, if you like.

For fried pizza, see the method on page 17

For the tray method
Follow the recipe instructions on page 19. The whole process will take about 90 minutes. Heat the oven to 260°C/gas mark 8 and stretch the dough to the edges of the tray. Be sure to spread your sauce right to the edges before adding toppings. The tray pizza dough serves 4, so quadruple the ingredient quantities. Bake for no less than 10 minutes.

The radicchio is bitter, the caramelised onion is sweet and the blue cheese is creamy and sharp, giving this pizza seriously strong and sensual flavours. It is advisable to eat this pizza when you are feeling very grown up.

RADICCHIO, CARAMELISED ONION, MOZZARELLA & PECORINO BAKED

ingredients, per pizza

1 dough ball (see page 16), left to rise for 1½–2 hours
flour, for dusting

for the radicchio (makes enough for 4 baked pizzas)
120g (16 leaves) radicchio
2 tablespoons extra virgin olive oil
generous pinch of salt

for the caramelised onion (makes enough for 4 baked pizzas)
1 large onion, thinly sliced
1 dessertspoon olive oil
1 teaspoon cane sugar
½ teaspoon vinegar

60g *mozzarella fior di latte*, torn into 5 chunks
5 teaspoons grated Pecorino
4 dessertspoons tomato sauce (see page 20)
2 teaspoons extra virgin olive oil

Prepare the radicchio: In a large bowl, mix the radicchio with the olive oil and salt and leave to marinate for 40 minutes.

Make the caramelised onion: Heat the olive oil in a frying pan over a low heat and sweat the onion for about 20 minutes. Add a little water if they start to stick. (If the onions burn, discard them.) When they have turned a golden colour, stir in the sugar and vinegar and reduce the temperature further. After about 15 minutes, the onions should have caramelised.

Place a rack on the highest shelf of an oven and turn the grill to its highest setting. When hot, place a greased 26cm iron pan on the stovetop, set to medium heat.

Sprinkle a little flour over your hands and on the work surface and open the dough ball by flattening and stretching the dough with your fingers, or by rolling the dough with a rolling pin. Pick the pizza base up and gently stretch it a little further over your fists without tearing it. Drop this onto the hot pan, and allow it to start rising.

As soon as the dough firms up, spread the tomato sauce over the base with the back of a metal spoon. Distribute a quarter of the caramelised onions on top, a quarter of the radicchio and then add the radicchio, mozzarella and Pecorino.

Cook the pizza on top of the stove for about 3 minutes, then transfer the pan to the grill for a further 3–4 minutes.

Serve whole or in slices.

Chorizo is a wonderful Iberian pork sausage, made with smoked red peppers (pimenton), which comes in both fresh and dried varieties. Countries as diverse as Hungary and Mexico make good versions of chorizo-like pork sausage. In fact, anywhere known for its smoked paprikas and chillies (or plant varieties of the genus *Capsicum*) often has pork products that are worth a try.

CHORIZO   BAKED OR TRAY

ingredients, per pizza

1 dough ball (see page 16),
    left to rise for
    1½ –2 hours OR
    dough 2 for tray pizzas
flour, for dusting

1 dessertspoon extra virgin
    olive oil
1 garlic clove, peeled and
    roughly chopped
4 dessertspoons tomato
    sauce (see page 20)
about 7 slices chorizo
6–8 chunks cooking
    chorizo
60g *mozzarella fior di
    latte*, torn into 5 chunks
4 basil leaves, torn
freshly ground black
    pepper

In a saucepan, heat the oil and fry the garlic over a low heat until lightly golden. Stir in the tomato sauce.

Place a rack on the highest shelf of an oven and turn the grill to its highest setting. When hot, place a greased 26cm iron pan on the stovetop, set to medium heat.

Sprinkle a little flour over your hands and on the work surface and open the dough ball by flattening and stretching the dough with your fingers, or by rolling the dough with a rolling pin. Pick the pizza base up and gently stretch it a little further over your fists without tearing it. Drop this onto the hot pan, and allow it to start rising.

As soon as the dough firms up, spread the tomato and garlic sauce over the base with the back of a metal spoon. Scatter the chorizo and mozzarella on top.

Cook the pizza on top of the stove for about 3 minutes, then transfer the pan to the grill for a further 3–4 minutes.

Once ready, scatter the basil leaves on top and serve with a few grinds of pepper, in one piece or sliced.

For the tray method
Follow the recipe instructions on page 19. The whole process will take about 90 minutes. Heat the oven to 260°C/gas mark 8 and stretch the dough to the edges of the tray. Be sure to spread your sauce right to the edges before adding toppings. The tray pizza dough serves 4, so quadruple the ingredient quantities. Bake for no less than 10 minutes.

INGREDIENT NOTE

Avoid boiled and smoked sausages and the less fatty varieties, but try products such as Calabrian *'nduja*. The fat runs as it cooks, becoming a tasty capsicum-infused oil, which makes a very juicy pizza.

This pizza is very satisfying. The blue cheese and pancetta work well together, and the sweet onion adds complexity. Though a little on the rich side, this pizza might well be recommended as the perfect hangover cure after a big night out.

PANCETTA, CARAMELISED
ONION & BLUE CHEESE BAKED OR TRAY

ingredients, per pizza

1 dough ball (see page 16),
   left to rise for
   1½ –2 hours OR
   dough 2 for tray pizzas
flour, for dusting

1 dessertspoon extra virgin
   olive oil
65g blue cheese, broken
   into 5 chunks
4 slices pancetta
60g *mozzarella fior di
   latte*, torn into 5 chunks

for the caramelised onion
   **(makes enough
   for 4 baked pizzas)**
1 large onions, thinly sliced
1 dessertspoon olive oil
1 teaspoon cane sugar
½ teaspoon vinegar

Make the caramelised onion: Heat the olive oil in a frying pan over a low heat and sweat the onion for about 20 minutes. Add a little water if they start to stick. (If the onions burn, discard them.) When they have turned a golden colour, stir in the sugar and vinegar and reduce the temperature further. After about 15 minutes, the onions should have caramelised.

Place a rack on the highest shelf of an oven and turn the grill to its highest setting. When hot, place a greased 26cm iron pan on the stovetop, set to medium heat.

Sprinkle a little flour over your hands and on the work surface and open the dough ball by flattening and stretching the dough with your fingers, or by rolling the dough with a rolling pin. Pick the pizza base up and gently stretch it a little further over your fists without tearing it. Drop this onto the hot pan, and allow it to start rising.

As soon as the dough firms up, drizzle the base with olive oil and distribute a quarter of the caramelised onion on top, then add the blue cheese, pancetta and mozzarella.

Cook the pizza on top of the stove for about 3 minutes, then transfer the pan to the grill for a further 3–4 minutes.

Serve whole or in slices.

For the tray method
Follow the recipe instructions on page 19. The whole process will take about 90 minutes. Heat the oven to 260°C/gas mark 8 and stretch the dough to the edges of the tray. Be sure to spread your sauce right to the edges before adding toppings. The tray pizza dough serves 4, so quadruple the ingredient quantities. Bake for no less than 10 minutes.

This pizza presents a subtle mix of flavours that works like a dream – the blue cheese is tangy and scented, the goat's cheese is austere, while the mozzarella and washed rind cheeses add creamy bass notes. The bitter, crunchy radicchio cuts through the richness of them all, making this an almost decadent but extremely delicious pizza.

MIXED CHEESE WITH RADICCHIO BAKED

ingredients, per pizza

1 dough ball (see page 16), left to rise for 1½ –2 hours

flour, for dusting

for the radicchio (makes enough for 4 baked pizzas)

150g (16 leaves) radicchio (*Tardivo*, if possible)

2 tablespoons extra virgin olive oil

generous pinch of salt

1 dessertspoon extra virgin olive oil

15g Ogleshield or washed rind cheese

15g goat's cheese, crumbled

20g blue cheese, crumbled

75g *mozzarella fior di latte*, torn into 6 chunks

4 basil leaves, torn

Prepare the radicchio: In a large bowl, mix the radicchio with the olive oil and salt and leave to marinate for 40 minutes.

Place a rack on the highest shelf of an oven and turn the grill to its highest setting. When hot, place a greased 26cm iron pan on the stovetop, set to medium heat.

Sprinkle a little flour over your hands and on the work surface and open the dough ball by flattening and stretching the dough with your fingers, or by rolling the dough with a rolling pin. Pick the pizza base up and gently stretch it a little further over your fists without tearing it. Drop this onto the hot pan, and allow it to start rising.

As soon as the dough firms up, drizzle the base with olive oil, then add all the cheeses, the basil and a quarter of the marinated radicchio leaves.

Cook the pizza on top of the stove for about 3 minutes, then transfer the pan to the grill for a further 3–4 minutes.

Serve whole or in slices.

INGREDIENT NOTE

In late winter/early spring you may find *Tardivo* (or to give it its full name: *Radicchio Rosso di Treviso Tardivo*), which is a very special sweet radicchio that looks a little like a tentacled octopus. If this is the case, slice it in half lengthways, rub with olive oil, salt and freshly milled pepper and sear it in a hot pan.

CHILLI OIL

OLIO AL PEPERONCINO

1 LITRE
400g scotch bonnet chillies (including seeds), chopped
20g paprika (optional)
200ml groundnut oil
800ml olive oil

Place the chillies, groundnut oil and paprika (if using – it will add colour) in a heavy sauté pan and warm over a very low heat – the oil should never be above 140°C – until the chillies have lost all their water content (about 30 minutes). The smoke from this will make you choke, so open the kitchen windows beforehand!

Remove the pan from the heat and add the olive oil. Allow to cool, then transfer to a covered container for 48 hours. Filter well through a sieve and store in sterilised bottles or jars in a cool, dark place for up to a year.

CHILLI PASTE

This is great for flavouring sausages or meatballs (see page 46). The best chillies to use are the red ones available towards the end of the season, when they are a little dry.

MAKES 200G
400g red chillies, cut into strips and seeds removed

Preheat the oven to 130°C/gas mark ½. Place the chillies skin-side down in a roasting tray, cover generously with water and bake in an oven for about 2 hours, until the water has evaporated. (Keep an eye on them to avoid browning.)

Reduce the oven temperature to 90°C and bake for a further 2 hours, by which time you will be left with a paste similar in consistency to that of tomato purée.

Pass the paste through a food mill using a sieve fine enough to retain the skin and the seeds, if any remain.

Bottle the paste in a sterilised, sealable container and store in a cool, dark place for up to a year.

Variation
You can make a non-hot version using red peppers instead of chillies, or a milder version using a mixture of red peppers and chillies. You could also try mixing large green ancho chillies with red chillies for a different flavour.

Goat's curd is light and has a good acidity that complements the meaty strength of the salami well. You need a soft salami, like *finocchiona* or even *ciauscolo* or *'nduja* – a spicy, spreadable sausage that you can add in small pieces. In Majorca, they make a very soft *sobrasada*, which is also very good for this pizza.

SALAMI & GOAT'S CURD BAKED

ingredients, per pizza

1 dough ball (see page 16),
  left to rise for
  1½–2 hours
flour, for dusting

4 dessertspoons tomato
  sauce (see page 20)
1 dessertspoon extra virgin
  olive oil
8 slices salami
60g *mozzarella fior di
  latte*, torn into 5 chunks
20g goat's curd, sliced
a handful of rocket or
  watercress
freshly ground black
  pepper
chilli oil, optional
  (see page 80)

Place a rack on the highest shelf of an oven and turn the grill to its highest setting. When hot, place a greased 26cm iron pan on the stovetop, set to medium heat.

Sprinkle a little flour over your hands and on the work surface and open the dough ball by flattening and stretching the dough with your fingers, or by rolling the dough with a rolling pin. Pick the pizza base up and gently stretch it a little further over your fists without tearing it. Drop this onto the hot pan, and allow it to start rising.

As soon as the dough firms up, spread the tomato sauce over the base using the back of a metal spoon. Drizzle with the olive oil and lay down the salami and mozzarella on top.

Cook the pizza on top of the stove for about 3 minutes, then transfer the pan to the grill for a further 3–4 minutes.

Once ready, spread the goat's curd evenly over the pizza, dress with rocket (or watercress in summer) and serve whole, with a grind of black pepper and more olive oil or chilli oil. The latter complements this recipe very well.

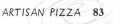

The flavours of this pizza are mild and sweet – perfect for a hot or breezy summer's day. The courgettes are cooked with mint, which complements their light sweetness, and the mild, cool goat's curd within the fresh courgette flowers contributes blissfully to this effect. The flowers themselves make a lovely decoration too.

COURGETTE, GRUYÈRE & GOAT'S CURD BAKED

ingredients, per pizza

1 dough ball (see page 16),
   left to rise for
   1¹/₂ –2 hours
flour, for dusting

for the courgettes
   **(makes enough
   for 4 baked pizzas)**
220g courgettes, thinly
   sliced
1 teaspoon olive oil
10 basil leaves, torn
a pinch of salt
5 mint leaves, chopped

for the courgette flowers
   **(makes enough
   for 4 baked pizzas)**
4 courgette flowers
4 tablespoons goat's curd
salt and freshly ground
   black pepper

1 dessertspoon extra virgin
   olive oil
4 basil leaves
30g Gruyère, sliced
60g *mozzarella fior di
   latte*, torn into 5 chunks

Prepare the courgettes: Place the courgettes in a wide, shallow pan and stir in the oil and basil. Place, covered, over a low heat for about 20 minutes. Season with salt and chopped mint.

Prepare the courgette flowers: Carefully unfurl the flower petals and spoon in 1 tablespoon seasoned goat's curd so that it holds its shape. Gently twist the petals to reseal the flower.

Place a rack on the highest shelf of an oven and turn the grill to its highest setting. When hot, place a greased 26cm iron pan on the stovetop, set to medium heat.

Sprinkle a little flour over your hands and on the work surface and open the dough ball by flattening and stretching the dough with your fingers, or by rolling the dough with a rolling pin. Pick the pizza base up and gently stretch it a little further over your fists without tearing it. Drop this onto the hot pan, and allow it to start rising.

As soon as the dough firms up, drizzle with the olive oil. Distribute a quarter of the courgettes evenly over the pizza, then add the basil, Gruyère and mozzarella.

Cook the pizza on top of the stove for about 3 minutes, then transfer the pan to the grill for a further 3–4 minutes.

Finish with a curd-filled courgette flower and serve whole or in slices.

A Caprese is similar to a Margherita pizza but uses
all the ingredients in their raw (and best) states,
like a wonderful Tricolore salad.

CAPRESE BAKED

ingredients, per pizza

1 dough ball (see page 16),
   left to rise for
   1 1/2 –2 hours
flour, for dusting

1 dessertspoon olive oil
1/2 teaspoon flaked sea salt
pinch of oregano
3 large, ripe, juicy
   tomatoes, sliced
70g buffalo mozzarella,
   sliced
4 basil leaves, torn
4 teaspoons basil-infused
   olive oil

Place a rack on the highest shelf of an oven and turn the grill to its highest setting. When hot, place a greased 26cm iron pan on the stovetop, set to medium heat.

Sprinkle a little flour over your hands and on the work surface and open the dough ball by flattening and stretching the dough with your fingers, or by rolling the dough with a rolling pin. Pick the pizza base up and gently stretch it a little further over your fists without tearing it. Drop this onto the hot pan, and allow it to start rising.

As soon as the dough firms up, drizzle the olive oil over the base and add the salt and a pinch of oregano.

Cook the pizza on top of the stove for about 3 minutes, then transfer the pan to the grill for a further 3–4 minutes.

Arrange the tomato slices, mozzarella and basil, alternately, in a circle over the base and drizzle with a little basil-infused olive oil.

Serve whole or in slices.

INGREDIENT NOTE

Basil pesto (see page 34) makes a tasty and decorative addition, but only if you have it to hand – this is a pizza designed for minimum fuss and maximum freshness.
   If you have very good tomatoes, and more time on your hands, try the Positanese recipe on page 119.

Smoked cheese makes an interesting alternative to mozzarella on pizzas, and you can purchase great smoked cheeses from many producers. If you want to try smoking cheese yourself, and you do not have a wood smoker, try tea-smoking in an ordinary domestic oven. We have suggested a way to do this, on page 23.

WILD MUSHROOM &
TEA-SMOKED CHEESE BAKED OR TRAY

ingredients, per pizza

1 dough ball (see page 16),
   left to rise for
   1½ –2 hours OR
   dough 2 for tray pizzas
flour, for dusting

for the wild mushrooms
   (makes enough
   for 4 baked pizzas)
160g wild mushrooms
2 dessertspoons extra
   virgin olive oil
2 dessertspoons butter
pinch of sea salt

1 dessertspoon olive oil
30g tea-smoked cheese
   (see page 23)
60g *mozzarella fior di
   latte*, torn into 5 chunks
4 basil leaves, torn

Prepare the wild mushrooms: Rub the mushrooms with a damp tea towel to remove any mulch. Do not soak them in water or they become slimy. Heat the olive oil and butter in a frying pan over a low heat and sear the mushrooms for about 3 minutes, seasoning with a pinch of salt.

Place a rack on the highest shelf of an oven and turn the grill to its highest setting. When hot, place a greased 26cm iron pan on the stovetop, set to medium heat.

Sprinkle a little flour over your hands and on the work surface and open the dough ball by flattening and stretching the dough with your fingers, or by rolling the dough with a rolling pin. Pick the pizza base up and gently stretch it a little further over your fists without tearing it. Drop this onto the hot pan, and allow it to start rising.

As soon as the dough firms up, drizzle the olive oil over the base. Add a quarter of the mushrooms, then scatter the smoked cheese, mozzarella and basil on top.

Cook the pizza on top of the stove for about 3 minutes, then transfer the pan to the grill for a further 3–4 minutes.

Serve whole or in slices.

For the tray method
Follow the recipe instructions on page 19. The whole process will take about 90 minutes. Heat the oven to 260°C/gas mark 8 and stretch the dough to the edges of the tray. Be sure to spread your sauce right to the edges before adding toppings. The tray pizza dough serves 4, so quadruple the ingredient quantities. Bake for no less than 10 minutes.

The sweet and pleasant flavour of butternut squash pairs well with a light, fresh goat's curd. As this is a simple pizza, it really highlights the quality of your ingredients so make sure you have a good olive oil if possible.

BUTTERNUT SQUASH & GOAT'S CURD BAKED

ingredients, per pizza

1 dough ball (see page 16),
    left to rise for
    1½ -2 hours
flour, for dusting

**for the butternut squash
    (makes enough
    for 4 baked pizzas)**
180g butternut squash,
    peeled and cut into
    small wedges
2 tablespoons olive oil
sea salt

1 dessertspoon extra virgin
    olive oil
65g *mozzarella fior di
    latte*, torn into 6 chunks
2 tablespoons goat's curd
basil pesto, optional
    (see page 34)

Prepare the butternut squash: Preheat the oven to 220°C/gas mark 7. Coat the wedges in the olive oil, sprinkle with salt and bake in the oven for 40 minutes, turning once. Reduce to 180°C/gas mark 4 after 20 minutes. By the end, the squash should be a sticky, caramelized, mashed consistency, not hard at all. Set aside.

Place a rack on the highest shelf of an oven and turn the grill to its highest setting. When hot, place a greased 26cm iron pan on the stovetop, set to medium heat.

Sprinkle a little flour over your hands and on the work surface and open the dough ball by flattening and stretching the dough with your fingers, or by rolling the dough with a rolling pin. Pick the pizza base up and gently stretch it a little further over your fists without tearing it. Drop this onto the hot pan, and allow it to start rising.

As soon as the dough firms up, spread the butternut mash onto the pizza with the back of a moistened metal spoon. Drizzle with olive oil and add the mozzarella. Dollop 1 tablespoon of curd around the top of the pizza.

Cook the pizza on top of the stove for about 3 minutes, then transfer the pan to the grill for a further 3–4 minutes.

Once ready, dress with the remainder of the curd and some basil pesto, if you like, and serve in pieces or whole.

INGREDIENT NOTE

An alternative method for preparing the butternut squash is to boil it in a little water for 10-15 minutes until cooked through. Then transfer to a bowl, add a little butter and salt and mash.

Spring, and particularly early spring in a southern climate, is the best season for artichokes. Artichoke season does not last long so eat as much of this delight as you can, while you can.

ARTICHOKES, NEW POTATOES & SPRING ONIONS TRAY

ingredients, per pizza

1 quantity dough 2
flour, for dusting

for the vegetable topping (makes enough for 4 baked pizzas)
2 tablespoons olive oil
400g spring onions, thinly sliced
80g firm, waxy new potatoes (eg Maris Piper), sliced in 1cm rounds
1 large globe artichoke, quartered (see box)
sea salt and freshly ground black pepper
several sprigs mint
flat-leaf parsley, chopped

2 tablespoons olive oil
80g *mozzarella fior di latte*, torn into 8 chunks
60g Parmiggiano reggiano, grated

This is a tray pizza (see page 19). Turn your oven to its highest setting and place a rack on the middle shelf.

Stretch the dough towards the edges of a 23.5 x 30cm oiled baking tray in 2 stages, resting for 10 minutes between each stretch.

Make the vegetable topping: Heat the oil in a wide, shallow pan and sweat the spring onions over a very low heat, to soften. Add the potatoes and artichoke quarters and add about ½ cup water. Sprinkle with ½ teaspoon salt, a few grinds of pepper, a few mint leaves and plenty of parsley. Cover and cook for 10 minutes. After 5 minutes, either remove the lid or continue to cook covered, depending on how fast the water is evaporating. Your aim is to cook off all the water.

Pour a little olive oil into the palm of your hand and pat it lightly over the top of the dough, making sure it touches the edges. Add the mozzarella and grate half the Parmesan over the base. Add the artichoke, potato and onion, distributing it evenly over the pizza.

Bake on the middle rack of your preheated oven for 12-14 minutes. If you have created a very thin pizza base, check for doneness after 10 minutes.

Once ready, sprinkle the remaining Parmesan on top and serve in slices.

INGREDIENT NOTE

To prepare the artichokes, remove the outer leaves and, with a sharp knife, remove the top spike and the hard skin of the stalk. Cut the artichoke lengthways and remove the hairs (too many denote a bad artichoke), then slice and rest in water with a squeeze of lemon juice to prevent oxidation.

This mix of aubergine, capers, garlic and pinenuts is also known as a *caponata* and is an Italian classic. It is well worth making extra as not only does it make a great pizza topping, but it's delicious as a salad or an accompaniment to baked fish.

AUBERGINE WITH CAPERS, ROASTED GARLIC & PINE NUTS (CAPONATA) BAKED OR FRIED

ingredients, per pizza

1 dough ball (see page 16),
    left to rise for
    1½ –2 hours
flour, for dusting

for the *caponata*:
    (makes enough
    for 4 baked pizzas)
4 teaspoons capers in salt
    (or large, good-quality
    capers in brine)
4 large garlic cloves,
    whole, unpeeled
4 teaspoons pine nuts
12 tablespoons extra virgin
    olive oil
2 large aubergines, cut
    into 4 thick slices,
    then cubed
16 basil leaves, torn

4 dessertspoons tomato
    sauce (see page 20)
3 basil leaves, torn
60g *mozzarella fior di
    latte*, torn into 5 chunks
olive oil, for drizzling

Make the caponata: Preheat the oven to 200°C/gas mark 6. Soak the capers in water for half an hour or so. If using the unsalted variety, simply wash well and dry off.

Roast the garlic in its skin for about 10 minutes, or until soft and brown. Roast the pine nuts in a hot pan, watching carefully that they do not burn. Peel the garlic and reserve. In a small frying pan, warm the oil over a low heat and fry the capers for about 10 minutes. Add the aubergine and cook until tender. Take the pan off the heat and add the pine nuts, garlic and basil. Set aside – the flavours will infuse as the mixture cools.

Place a rack on the highest shelf of an oven and turn the grill to its highest setting. When hot, place a greased 26cm iron pan on the stovetop, set to medium heat.

Sprinkle a little flour over your hands and on the work surface and open the dough ball by flattening and stretching the dough with your fingers, or by rolling the dough with a rolling pin. Pick the pizza base up and gently stretch it a little further over your fists without tearing it. Drop this onto the hot pan, and allow it to start rising.

As soon as the dough firms up, spread the tomato sauce over the base with the back of a metal spoon. Distribute 2 tablespoons of *caponata* evenly over the top and finish with the basil, mozzarella and a drizzle of olive oil.

Cook the pizza on top of the stove for about 3 minutes, then transfer the pan to the grill for a further 3–4 minutes.

Once ready, serve with an extra spoonful of *caponata* and chunk of mozzarella on the side.

For fried pizza, see the method on page 17

Ricotta is sometimes in danger of being a little bland (as opposed to subtle). However, the less fat in the milk, the closer the ricotta is to yogurt, giving it an interesting 'tang'. The best ricotta is usually sheep's milk ricotta, followed by buffalo, then cow.

COURGETTE & RICOTTA BAKED OR FRIED

ingredients, per pizza

1 dough ball (see page 16),
   left to rise for
   1½–2 hours
flour, for dusting

for the courgettes
   (makes enough
   for 4 baked pizzas)
240g courgettes, thinly
   sliced
1 tablespoon olive oil
10 basil leaves, torn
5 mint leaves, finely
   chopped

for the *crema di ricotta*:
   (makes enough
   for 1 baked pizza)
2 teaspoons milk
4 dessertspoons ricotta
sea salt

1 dessertspoon extra virgin
   olive oil
4 basil leaves, torn
60g *mozzarella fior di
   latte*, torn into 5 chunks
4 teaspoons grated
   Pecorino

Prepare the courgettes: Place the courgettes in a wide, shallow pan and stir in the oil and basil. Place, covered, over a low heat for about 20 minutes. Season with salt and chopped mint.

Make the crema di ricotta: In a bowl, stir the milk into the ricotta and mix to a smooth consistency. Season with salt and pepper to taste.

Place a rack on the highest shelf of an oven and turn the grill to its highest setting. When hot, place a greased 26cm iron pan on the stovetop, set to medium heat.

Sprinkle a little flour over your hands and on the work surface and open the dough ball by flattening and stretching the dough with your fingers, or by rolling the dough with a rolling pin. Pick the pizza base up and gently stretch it a little further over your fists without tearing it. Drop this onto the hot pan, and allow it to start rising.

As soon as the dough firms up, spread the *crema di ricotta* over the base with the back of a metal spoon. Drizzle over the olive oil and distribute the courgettes and basil evenly over the surface. Finish with the mozzarella and grated Pecorino.

Cook the pizza on top of the stove for about 3 minutes, then transfer the pan to the grill for a further 3–4 minutes.

Once ready, dress with the remaining Pecorino and serve whole or in slices.

For fried pizza, see the method on page 17

INGREDIENT NOTE

When you buy your courgettes, try to find courgette flowers at the same time, as then you can stuff them with ricotta, wrap them in dough, deep fry the whole flower and enjoy as an appetiser.

Chorizo is a strong cured meat with plenty of flavour and spicy aroma. When you contrast this with a fresh, mild cheese such as ricotta, and throw in plenty of crunchy green watercress to balance it off, you are in no danger of adulterating its deep umami.

CHORIZO WITH RICOTTA & WATERCRESS BAKED

ingredients, per pizza

1 dough ball (see page 16),
  left to rise for
  1¹/₂–2 hours
flour, for dusting

for the *crema di ricotta*:
  (makes enough
  for 1 baked pizza)
2 teaspoons milk
4 dessertspoons ricotta
sea salt

1 dessertspoon extra virgin
  olive oil
6 slices chorizo
6 chunks cooking chorizo,
  skinned and broken
60g *mozzarella fior di
  latte*, torn into 5 chunks
4 basil leaves, torn
a small handful of
  watercress, washed
  and dried

Make the crema di ricotta: In a bowl, stir the milk into the ricotta and mix to a smooth consistency. Season with salt and pepper to taste.

Place a rack on the highest shelf of an oven and turn the grill to its highest setting. When hot, place a greased 26cm iron pan on the stovetop, set to medium heat.

Sprinkle a little flour over your hands and on the work surface and open the dough ball by flattening and stretching the dough with your fingers, or by rolling the dough with a rolling pin. Pick the pizza base up and gently stretch it a little further over your fists without tearing it. Drop this onto the hot pan, and allow it to start rising.

As soon as the dough firms up, turn the heat down to medium and drizzle with the olive oil. Spread the *crema di ricotta* over the base with the back of a metal spoon. Add both types of chorizo and the mozzarella and distribute the basil leaves on top.

Cook the pizza on top of the stove for about 3 minutes, then transfer the pan to the grill for a further 3–4 minutes.

Once ready, finish with a mound of watercress. Serve whole.

Italians appreciate and take great pride in the authentic flavours of their respective regions. They celebrate the fruits of their various terroirs by producing wines, cheeses and diverse regional products, many of which have acquired international renown.

Capers, olives and anchovies are crucial to the gastronomy of Southern Italy. Around Naples, where the iconic *Pizza Alla Napoletana* was born, these three ingredients feature significantly, both together and apart, in many signature dishes and recipes.

NEOPOLITAN BAKED OR FRIED

ingredients, per pizza

1 dough ball (see page 16), left to rise for 1¹/₂–2 hours
flour, for dusting

8 capers in salt
1 garlic clove, peeled and roughly chopped
2 tablespoons olive oil
4 dessertspoons tomato sauce (see page 20)
1 teaspoon oregano
4 anchovy fillets
5 kalamata olives, a mixture of black and green
4 basil leaves, torn (plus more to serve)
60g *mozzarella fior di latte*, torn into 5 chunks

Wash the salted capers and soak them in plenty of water for at least 1 hour, then drain.

Fry the garlic in 1 tablespoon of the olive oil until lightly golden, then stir in the tomato sauce.

Place a rack on the highest shelf of an oven and turn the grill to its highest setting. When hot, place a greased 26cm iron pan on the stovetop, set to medium heat.

Sprinkle a little flour over your hands and on the work surface and open the dough ball by flattening and stretching the dough with your fingers, or by rolling the dough with a rolling pin. Pick the pizza base up and gently stretch it a little further over your fists without tearing it. Drop this onto the hot pan, and allow it to start rising.

As soon as the dough firms up in the hot pan, spread the tomato and garlic sauce over the base with the back of a metal spoon. Sprinkle over the oregano and the remaining olive oil.

Distribute the anchovies, olives, capers and basil leaves evenly over the surface and scatter the cheese on top.

Cook the pizza on top of the stove for about 3 minutes, then transfer the pan to the grill for a further 3–4 minutes.

Once ready, decorate with more basil and serve in one piece or sliced.

For fried pizza, see the method on page 17

This is a lovely vegetarian pizza that enhances a signature vegetable (spinach) with the simple addition of butter and a good, sharp cheese.

SPINACH, BUTTER & PECORINO BAKED

ingredients, per pizza

1 dough ball (see page 16), left to rise for 1½–2 hours
flour, for dusting

for the spinach (makes enough for 4 baked pizzas)

2 teaspoons extra virgin olive oil
1 garlic clove, crushed
260g spinach
sea salt and freshly ground black pepper

for the *crema di ricotta* (makes enough for 1 baked pizza)

2 teaspoons milk
4 dessertspoons ricotta
sea salt

1 dessertspoon extra virgin olive oil
60g *mozzarella fior di latte*, torn into 5 chunks
a few dabs of butter
4 teaspoons grated Pecorino

Prepare the spinach: Heat the oil in a wide, shallow pan and fry the garlic. Add the leaves, some salt and a drop of water and cover. Cook for about 4 minutes. Drain well and squeeze excess water from the leaves before using.

Make the crema di ricotta: In a bowl, stir the milk into the ricotta and mix to a smooth consistency. Season with salt and pepper to taste.

Place a rack on the highest shelf of an oven and turn the grill to its highest setting. When hot, place a greased 26cm iron pan on the stovetop, set to medium heat.

Sprinkle a little flour over your hands and on the work surface and open the dough ball by flattening and stretching the dough with your fingers, or by rolling the dough with a rolling pin. Pick the pizza base up and gently stretch it a little further over your fists without tearing it. Drop this onto the hot pan, and allow it to start rising.

As soon as the dough firms up, spread the *crema di ricotta* over the base using the back of a metal spoon. Drizzle over the olive oil and add the spinach and mozzarella.

Cook the pizza on top of the stove for about 3 minutes, then transfer the pan to the grill for a further 3–4 minutes.

Once ready, drop dabs of soft butter onto the pizza and sprinkle the grated Pecorino on top. Serve whole or in slices.

Try, if you can, to find Gloucester Old Spot pancetta, as it's one of the best. Alternatively, look for a pancetta that has been rolled in mountain herbs as these add an extra dimension of flavour. Bacon will do, but definitely takes second place to a well-produced sweet pancetta. Or you could drop the meat altogether, as spinach, olives and smoked mozzarella make a lovely vegetarian option.

PANCETTA, SPINACH, OLIVES & SMOKED CHEESE BAKED

ingredients, per pizza

1 dough ball (see page 16), left to rise for 1¹/₂ –2 hours
flour, for dusting

for the spinach (makes enough for 1 baked pizza)
2 teaspoons extra virgin olive oil
1 garlic clove, crushed
¹/₂ red chilli, finely chopped (optional)
260g spinach
sea salt

1 dessertspoon extra virgin olive oil
4 kalamata olives
60g *mozzarella fior di latte*, torn into 5 chunks
25g smoked buffalo mozzarella, torn into 3 chunks
4 slices pancetta
Pecorino or Parmesan, to serve

Prepare the spinach: Heat a little oil in a pan and fry the chilli and garlic. Add the leaves, some salt and a drop of water and cover. Cook for about 4 minutes. Drain well and squeeze excess water from the leaves before using.

Place a rack on the highest shelf of an oven and turn the grill to its highest setting. When hot, place a greased 26cm iron pan on the stovetop, set to medium heat.

Sprinkle a little flour over your hands and on the work surface and open the dough ball by flattening and stretching the dough with your fingers, or by rolling the dough with a rolling pin. Pick the pizza base up and gently stretch it a little further over your fists without tearing it. Drop this onto the hot pan, and allow it to start rising.

As soon as the dough firms up, drizzle over the olive oil. Spread the spinach over the base and add the olives, both types of mozzarella and the pancetta.

Cook the pizza on top of the stove for about 3 minutes, then transfer the pan to the grill for a further 3–4 minutes.

Once ready, sprinkle with fresh shavings of Parmesan or Pecorino and serve whole or in slices.

INGREDIENT NOTE

Black olives are better than green for pizza, or a mix for Puttanesca (see page 109). Green olives are picked earlier (before ripening) and are generally firmer – hence better for eating fresh, or in salads. We particularly like the meaty flavour of Kalamata olives.

Though a little difficult to prepare, the artichoke core really is the heart of the matter and its rich, creamy texture needs only a little fresh mozzarella and olive oil to set it off. However, the potent tomato addition here delivers that extra deep, sun-dried flavour and brings all the elements in this pizza together.

ARTICHOKE, WITH SUN-DRIED TOMATOES, PARMESAN & BUFFALO MOZZARELLA BAKED

ingredients, per pizza

1 dough ball (see page 16),
   left to rise for
   1¹/₂ –2 hours
flour, for dusting

1 dessertspoon extra virgin
   olive oil
3 sundried tomatoes,
   sliced
1 artichoke heart,
   quartered
4 teaspoons grated
   Parmesan
60g buffalo mozzarella,
   torn into 5 chunks
sea salt and freshly ground
   black pepper

Place a rack on the highest shelf of an oven and turn the grill to its highest setting. When hot, place a greased 26cm iron pan on the stovetop, set to medium heat.

Sprinkle a little flour over your hands and on the work surface and open the dough ball by flattening and stretching the dough with your fingers, or by rolling the dough with a rolling pin. Pick the pizza base up and gently stretch it a little further over your fists without tearing it. Drop this onto the hot pan, and allow it to start rising.

As soon as the dough firms up, drizzle the base with olive oil and lay the sun-dried tomatoes and artichoke on top. Sprinkle with half the Parmesan cheese.

Cook the pizza on top of the stove for about 3 minutes, then transfer the pan to the grill for a further 3–4 minutes.

Once ready, finish with mounds of fresh buffalo mozzarella, season and finish with the remaining Parmesan.

INGREDIENT NOTE

See page 93 for how to prepare artichokes. However, if you want to save time, chargrilled artichokes bottled in oil are a perfectly fine alternative.

As with all ham products, it is best to choose the fattier cuts and varieties as the thinly sliced fats melt easily and moisten the pizza dough. This is especially tasty on a bianca pizza, where there's no tomato sauce.

PARMA HAM, PECORINO & ROCKET BAKED

ingredients, per pizza

1 dough ball (see page 16), left to rise for 1½ –2 hours

flour, for dusting

1 dessertspoon extra virgin olive oil

4-5 cherry tomatoes, halved

1 teaspoon sea salt

60g *mozzarella fior di latte*, torn into 5 chunks

4 slices Senese ham (or Parma)

4 teaspoons Pecorino, grated

50g buffalo mozzarella, torn into 4 chunks (optional)

a handful of rocket

Place a rack on the highest shelf of an oven and turn the grill to its highest setting. When hot, place a greased 26cm iron pan on the stovetop, set to medium heat.

Sprinkle the salt over the cherry tomatoes and set aside.

Sprinkle a little flour over your hands and on the work surface and open the dough ball by flattening and stretching the dough with your fingers, or by rolling the dough with a rolling pin. Pick the pizza base up and gently stretch it a little further over your fists without tearing it. Drop this onto the hot pan, and allow it to start rising.

As soon as the dough firms up, drizzle the base with olive oil. Lay the cherry tomatoes face down, then add the mozzarella and ham slices on top and sprinkle with half the Pecorino.

Cook the pizza on top of the stove for about 3 minutes, then transfer the pan to the grill for a further 3–4 minutes.

Finish with mounds of fresh buffalo mozzarella and a handful of rocket leaves, and sprinkle with the remaining Pecorino.

This recipe is a nod to the classic pasta sauce traditionally served with spaghetti, which takes advantage of fresh summer tomatoes and Italy's all-year signature ingredients: olives, capers and garlic.

PUTTANESCA BAKED OR TRAY

ingredients, per pizza

1 dough ball (see page 16), left to rise for 1½ –2 hours OR dough 2 for tray pizzas

flour, for dusting

**for the salsa
(makes enough
for 8 baked pizzas)**

400g fresh tomatoes

1 teaspoon salt

1 garlic clove, crushed

4 basil leaves, chopped

4 teaspoons salted capers

2 tablespoons olive oil

½ garlic clove, finely chopped

chilli, finely sliced

6-8 black and green olives on the stone, stoned and chopped

80g *mozzarella fior di latte*, torn into 6 chunks

½ teaspoon dried oregano

3 basil leaves, torn

freshly ground black pepper

Make the salsa: Soak the salted capers in plenty of water for at least 1 hour, then drain. Place the tomatoes in a pot of boiling water, remove from the stove and leave for about 3 minutes. Peel, de-seed and finely chop the tomatoes, then transfer to a sieve, salt and drain for about 20 minutes. Transfer the tomatoes to a bowl with the garlic and basil.

In a saucepan, over a low heat, cook the garlic, chilli, capers and olives in 1 tablespoon olive oil, until the garlic starts to brown. Keep warm.

Place a rack on the highest shelf of an oven and turn the grill to its highest setting. When hot, place a greased 26cm iron pan on the stovetop, set to medium heat.

Sprinkle a little flour over your hands and on the work surface and open the dough ball by flattening and stretching the dough with your fingers, or by rolling the dough with a rolling pin. Pick the pizza base up and gently stretch it a little further over your fists without tearing it. Drop this onto the hot pan, and allow it to start rising.

As soon as the dough firms up, spread half the tomato salsa over the base with the back of a metal spoon. Add the mozzarella, a sprinkle of oregano and a drizzle of olive oil.

Cook the pizza on top of the stove for about 3 minutes, then transfer the pan to the grill for a further 3–4 minutes.

Combine the rest of the tomatoes with the pan-fried mixture and some basil. Add to the baked pizza when it comes out the oven with a grind or two of black pepper. Serve whole or in slices.

For the tray method

Follow the recipe instructions on page 19. The whole process will take about 90 minutes. Heat the oven to 260°C/gas mark 8 and stretch the dough to the edges of the tray. Be sure to spread your sauce right to the edges before adding toppings. The tray pizza dough serves 4, so quadruple the ingredient quantities. Bake for no less than 10 minutes.

There is, arguably, nothing better than fresh asparagus spears bursting with moisture and earthy seasonal flavour. Together with fresh mozzarella and the purity of the best Parmesan Reggiano, this simple pizza is a spring treat.

ASPARAGUS & BUFFALO MOZZARELLA BAKED

ingredients, per pizza

1 dough ball (see page 16),
 left to rise for
 1½–2 hours
flour, for dusting

12 asparagus spears,
 trimmed
1 dessertspoon extra virgin
 olive oil
60g *mozzarella fior di
 latte*, torn into 5 chunks
a few dabs of butter
50g buffalo mozzarella,
 torn into 5 chunks
Parmesan shavings
a few basil leaves, torn

Place a rack on the highest shelf of an oven and turn the grill to its highest setting. When hot, place a greased 26cm iron pan on the stovetop, set to medium heat.

Bring a little water to the boil in a wide-bottomed pan, then steam the asparagus for a couple of minutes. A lid will help this along more thoroughly, but otherwise turn them once, then drain.

Sprinkle a little flour over your hands and on the work surface and open the dough ball by flattening and stretching the dough with your fingers, or by rolling the dough with a rolling pin. Pick the pizza base up and gently stretch it a little further over your fists without tearing it. Drop this onto the hot pan, and allow it to start rising.

As soon as the dough firms up, drizzle the olive oil over the base. Lay the asparagus over the pizza and distribute the mozzarella evenly.

Cook the pizza on top of the stove for about 3 minutes, then transfer the pan to the grill for a further 3–4 minutes.

Dress the pizza with a little butter, the bufffalo mozzarella and a few Parmesan shavings and torn basil leaves. Serve whole or in slices.

INGREDIENT NOTE

Divide the dough into smaller balls to make two little pizzas, as pictured, or any size you prefer.

Leeks go very well with potatoes and Cheddar cheese works well with both. This pizza is designed to have an authentic British character, taking advantage as it does of ingredients that are popular and available in the UK.

LEEK, POTATO & CHEDDAR TRAY

1 quantity tray dough
flour, for dusting

for the vegetable topping
30g unsalted butter
400g spring onion,
   thinly sliced
50g onion, thinly sliced
400g leek, thinly sliced
60g potatoes, sliced into
   ½ cm-thick rounds
freshly ground black
   pepper

1 tablespoon olive oil
50g *mozzarella fior di
   latte*, sliced
80g extra mature Cheddar
a few sprigs of flat-leaf
   parsley, chopped

This is a tray pizza (see page 19). Turn your oven to its highest setting and place a rack on the middle shelf.

Stretch the dough towards the edges of a 23.5 x 30cm oiled baking tray in 2 stages, resting for 10 minutes between each stretch.

Make the vegetable topping: Melt the butter in a wide-bottomed pan over a very low heat and sweat the spring onion and leek until tender – avoid browning. Add the potatoes and 110ml water, then cover and cook for 10 minutes. After 5 minutes, either remove the lid or continue to cook covered, depending on how fast the water is evaporating. Your aim is to cook off all the water.

Pour a little olive oil into the palm of your hand and pat it lightly over the top of the dough, making sure it touches the edges. Add the sliced mozzarella, the onion and potato mixture and grate the Cheddar on top.

Bake on the middle rack of your pre-heated oven for about 10 minutes. If you have created a very thin pizza base, check for doneness after 10 minutes.

Once ready, decorate with a little chopped parsley and serve in 4 slices.

ROSEMARY & SEA SALT FOCCACCIA

An unadulterated tray pizza (without tomato, cheese or other meats and veg) makes a great bread for the table or for sandwiches. Use a smaller tray, so you increase the height of the dough.

1 quantity tray dough (see page 19)
1 dessertspoon olive oil
sea salt, crushed
1 branch rosemary, sprigs removed

Turn your oven on to its highest setting. Follow the method for the tray pizza dough on page 19, and start with your dough stretched out to meet the sides of an oiled tray.

Pour the olive oil into the palm of your hand and pat it lightly over the top of the dough, making sure it touches the edges. Dimple the dough with your fingertips and add a little more oil. Sprinkle the crushed sea salt on top and gently push the rosemary into the dimples, without degassing the dough in too many places. (You can also mix slightly roasted, crushed rosemary into the dough beforehand and just finish with salt and olive oil.)

Bake in the oven for 8–10 minutes. Once ready, leave to cool. This can be served as a fresh bread, or left to stale slightly and used for bruschette.

BRUSCHETTA

Slice the focaccia (see method above) into desired lengths about 1cm wide. Toast and add toppings of your choice. All of the tray-baked pizza toppings can also be used for bruschetta but here are a few more ideas:

Garlic butter – Mash a few cloves of fresh garlic with softened butter and a few sprigs of chopped parsley and spread onto the bruschetta while hot.

Napoletana – Finely chop a mix of capers, olives and anchovies to make a salty tapenade and spread on hot bruschetta.

Pesto – See page 34.

These pizzette make a fresh and colourful summer treat as the toppings are all added after the dough has been fried. Also, being quick and simple to prepare, they make excellent canapés.

PIZZETTE *FRIED*

ingredients, (makes 8 canape pizzas or 16 pizzette)

1 quantity dough 1
(see page 17)
flour, for dusting

200g tomato sauce
(see page 20)
200ml groundnut or
vegetable oil
240g *mozzarella fior
di latte* or buffalo
mozzarella, torn into
small chunks
80g Parmesan, grated
10 basil leaves, shredded
sea salt and freshly ground
black pepper

Divide the dough into 8 or 16 pieces (depending on whether you want to make canape pizzas or pizzette). Shape these into round balls, cover and leave to rise for an hour in a warm place.

Heat the tomato sauce in a saucepan and bring to a simmer over a low heat to reduce for about 6 minutes. (This is important to enhance the flavour as the sauce is not cooked with the dough). Keep warm.

Sprinkle a little flour over your hands and on the work surface and open the dough balls by flattening and stretching the dough with your fingers, or by rolling the dough with a rolling pin.

Heat the oil in a deep, wide saucepan on a medium heat.

Gently, without tearing, stretch the dough with your fingertips. Drop this onto the hot oil, and allow to start rising. Turn the heat down if necessary – do not brown the pizzette, they should be golden. In batches, fry for a couple of minutes, turning once or twice.

Add the mozzarella, a sprinkle of Parmesan and a basil garnish, and then top with the hot tomato sauce and season to taste.

Other recipes we recommend you use for pizzette can be found on pages 32, 72, 94, 97 and 101.

This raw salsa is a classic from Positano on the Amalfi coast. You need very good tomatoes for this, so make sure that you find some that are super sweet and fruity. We also call this pizza 'a la Eduardo', a reference to Eduardo di Filippo, the famous Italian actor, playwright, author and poet, who passed this recipe on to us many years ago.

POSITANESE BAKED

ingredients, per pizza

1 dough ball (see page 16),
  left to rise for
  1¹/₂–2 hours
flour, for dusting

for the salsa
  (makes enough
  for 4 pizzas)
250g tomatoes
¹/₂ teaspoon salt
1 garlic clove, crushed
¹/₂ tablespoon mashed
  onion
30g olive oil
4 basil leaves
a pinch of dried oregano
a pinch of marjoram
a few sprigs of fresh
  parsley, chopped
1 tablespoon chopped
  celery (strings removed)
freshly ground black
  pepper

Parmesan, grated

Make the salsa: Bring a pot of water to the boil and remove from the stove. Place the tomatoes in the water and leave for about 3 minutes until their skins start to wrinkle. Peel and deseed the tomatoes and finely chop.

Place the tomatoes in a sieve, add the salt and leave to drain over a bowl for about 20 minutes. Discard the juice and transfer the drained tomatoes to a large bowl with the garlic.

Add all the remaining salsa ingredients and stir to combine. Marinate for at least 2 hours (it will keep in the fridge for up to 2 days, though if you do this, bring it up to room temperature before use).

Place a rack on the highest shelf of an oven and turn the grill to its highest setting. When hot, place a greased 26cm iron pan on the stovetop, set to medium heat.

Divide the salsa into two bowls and set one aside, reserving for later (in total, ensure you have enough for about 4 tablespoons per pizza).

Sprinkle a little flour over your hands and on the work surface and open the dough ball by flattening and stretching the dough with your fingers, or by rolling the dough with a rolling pin. Pick the pizza base up and gently stretch it a little further over your fists without tearing it. Drop this onto the hot pan, and allow it to start rising.

As soon as the dough firms up, spread a quarter of the tomato salsa over the base with the back of a metal spoon.

Cook the pizza on top of the stove for about 3 minutes, then transfer the pan to the grill for a further 3–4 minutes.

Once ready, add 2 tablespoons of the reserved salsa (at room temperature) and finish with Parmesan, either grated or shaved, with extra basil if you like. Serve whole or in slices.

The radicchio is essential to this recipe as its wonderful bitterness perfectly offsets the fatty sweetness of the cured pig's cheek. It retains some texture too, so its crunch also offsets the cheese. Our favourite kinds of radicchio are the *Treviggiana* varieties, from the Treviso area of Italy. These can be roasted or grilled to the point of caramelisation.

RADDICCHIO, SMOKED MOZZARELLA & PIG'S CHEEK   BAKED

ingredients, per pizza

1 dough ball (see page 16),
    left to rise for
    1½–2 hours
flour, for dusting

for the radicchio
    (makes enough
    for 4 pizzas)
120g (about 24 leaves)
    radicchio leaves
    (preferably Treviggiana)
2 tablespoons extra virgin
    olive oil
generous pinch of salt

1 dessertspoon extra virgin
    olive oil (or lard)
4 slices pig's cheek, sliced
4 basil leaves, torn
30g smoked mozzarella,
    torn into 4 chunks
4 teaspoons grated
    Parmesan
sea salt and freshly ground
    black pepper
60g buffalo mozzarella,
    torn into 5 chunks

Prepare the radicchio: In a large bowl, mix the radicchio with the olive oil and salt and leave to marinate for 40 minutes.

Place a rack on the highest shelf of an oven and turn the grill to its highest setting. When hot, place a greased 26cm iron pan on the stovetop, set to medium heat.

Sprinkle a little flour over your hands and on the work surface and open the dough ball by flattening and stretching the dough with your fingers, or by rolling the dough with a rolling pin. Pick the pizza base up and gently stretch it a little further over your fists without tearing it. Drop this onto the hot pan, and allow it to start rising.

As soon as the dough firms up, drizzle over the olive oil or lard. Arrange the pig's cheek on top, then add the radicchio, basil and smoked mozzarella. Scatter half the Parmesan on top.

Cook the pizza on top of the stove for about 3 minutes, then transfer the pan to the grill for a further 3–4 minutes.

Once ready, finish with a few clumps of the fresh, soft buffalo mozzarella, then season and sprinkle with the remaining Parmesan.

THE SEASONS

If buying ingredients can be fun, growing your own produce is even more rewarding. It also puts you in touch with the seasons and allows recipes to be determined by what is at its peak, in terms of juiciness, colour, texture and flavour and therefore often enhances the quality and the experience all round. Get into it!

HERBS

ERBE

Herbs are very easy to grow in pots and are fundamental ingredients to have on hand to add that extra fresh dimension to your cooking. For good seed suppliers, see the Resources section overleaf.

Basil
Basil is considered, correctly, an essential ingredient for pizza. The best basil to use is sweet *Ocimum Basilicum* 'Napoletano' or 'Lettuce Leaf Basil', though *Ocimum minimum* or 'Greek Basil' is another good choice. Basil grows well in pots – it likes a sunny window ledge or greenhouse – and adapts to most soils, though it is prone to slug and snail attacks.

Flat-Leaf Parsley
Parsley is a very versatile plant to have to hand and, being hardy, will survive most of the year. We recommend 'Japanese Parsley' for its distinctive flavour with strong hints of celery. It's a perennial so won't need to be replanted and should have leaves most of the year. You can also add the roots and young stems to salads. It grows well in the shade but does not like hot weather.

Oregano
Oregano vulgare is a hardy plant and well worth growing. It's also worth looking out for Cretan oregano seeds. This is a very small plant that grows in the high Cretan mountains and can withstand freezing temperatures, but does not like too much water. Plant in a very well drained soil in full sun.

Mint
Mint is a great, all-year herb and the non-invasive varieties grow well in pots. It goes particularly well with courgette and lamb pizza toppings and of course in almost any kind of salad.

Rocket
Rocket, or *muralis*, is traditionally collected from the wild – it grows in wall cracks (where lizards help carry the seeds). However, it can also be cultivated and simply requires plenty of drainage and good sun.

TOMATOES

POMODORI

Tomatoes are also good to grow as industrially farmed types are often lacking in flavour. The best kind are the 'heirloom' or 'heritage' varieties that have been cultivated over several generations for particular characteristics. We recommend the early-ripening, cold-tolerant 'Stupice', which does not even need training, and also the beautiful bright red 'Zapotec', which hates cold weather. The oddly named 'Orange Banana' is also worth growing as it can produce fruit well into the autumn and even early winter and makes a tasty, orangey passata.

VEGETABLES

VERDURE

Our pizza recipes make the most of a wide range of vegetables so if you have a garden to grow your own produce, it's well worth the effort. Here is a breakdown of the pizzas by season so you know what to grow (and what to eat) when:

SPRING *asparagus, leek, potato, spinach, artichoke*

pesto with baked potato & parmesan p. 33
spinach, caramelised onion, goat's cheese & stilton p. 61
smoked mozzarella, baked potato & pig's cheek p. 66
artichokes, new potatoes & spring onions p. 93
spinach, butter & pecorino p. 102
pancetta, spinach, olives & smoked cheese p. 105
artichoke, with sun-dried tomatoes, parmesan & buffalo mozzarella p. 107
asparagus & buffalo mozzarella p. 110
leek, potato & cheddar p. 113

SUMMER *courgette, aubergine, cherry tomato*

bresaola, cherry tomatoes & buffalo mozzarella p. 29
pancetta & aubergine p. 31
scorched red & yellow peppers p. 52
pork sausage, roasted peppers & parmesan p. 58
salami, smoked buffalo cheese & cherry tomatoes p. 65
courgette, gruyère & goat's curd p. 86
caprese p. 87
aubergine with capers, roasted garlic & pine nuts p. 94
courgette & ricotta p. 97
positanese p. 119

AUTUMN *wild mushroom, pepper, butternut squash*

ham, mushroom & ricotta p. 42
wild mushroom p. 72
wild mushroom & tea-smoked cheese p. 88
butternut squash & goat's curd p. 91

WINTER *pumpkin, broccoli/ turnip tops, radicchio*

broccoli, olive & smoked mozzarella p. 45
treviggiana reggiano, stilton & radicchio p. 53
sausage with wild broccoli p. 55
stilton, butternut squash & pine nuts p. 64
radicchio, caramelised onion, goat's cheese & stilton p. 73
mixed cheese with radicchio p. 72
raddicchio, smoked mozzarella & pig's cheek p. 121

RESOURCES

Franco Manca

Our chain of pizza restaurants. There are currently branches in Brixton, Battersea, Balham, Chiswick and Westfield in Stratford, London.

BRIXTON Unit 4, Market Row SW9 8LD
020 7738 3021

BATTERSEA 76 Northcote Road SW11 6QL
020 7924 3110

BALHAM 53 Bedford Hill SW12 9EZ
020 8772 0489

CHISWICK 144 Chiswick High Road W4 1PU
020 7738 3021

WESTFIELD Unit 2003, The Balcony, Westfield Stratford City E20 1ES
020 8522 6669

www.francomanca.com

CHEESE

Alham Wood Organics

A buffalo farm that produce a range of cheeses from their herd. Their products can be bought at various markets – see their website for details.

www.buffalo-organics.co.uk

Green's of Glastonbury

A Somerset cheesemaking dynasty that has been making traditional farmhouse cheeses for four generations. See their website for stockists.

www.greensofglastonbury.co.uk

Laverstoke Park Farm

An organic/biodynamic farm in Hampshire. Their products can be bought online – see their website for details.

www.laverstokepark.co.uk

Colton Bassett Dairy

Makers of Colton Bassett Stilton, used in Franco Manca restaurants. See website for UK and international stockists.

www.coltonbassettdairy.co.uk

Montgomery Cheese

Makers of Montgomery Cheddar and Ogleshield, both of which are used at Franco Manca restaurants.

www.montgomerycheese.co.uk

Stichelton Dairy

Makers of Stichelton, a British blue cheese used in the Franco Manca restaurants. See website for details.

www.stichelton.co.uk

The Fine Cheese Co.

Supplier of a wide range of cheeses including buffalo mozzarella, Pecorino, Gruyère and Parmesan.

www.finecheese.co.uk

EQUIPMENT

Nisbets

A great online resource for cooking equipment and supplies – baking trays, thermometers, scales, sausage machines, you name it.

www.nisbets.co.uk

GENERAL

Just So Italian

Suppliers of a wide selection of meats, cheese and storecupboard products.

www.justsoitalian.co.uk

Natoora

Wide range of quality Italian foods, including cheeses, meats and oils.

www.natoora.co.uk

La Piccola Deli

Imports the best foods direct from Italy (a good source of friarielli in cans). Delis in Kensington and Maida Vale. See website for details.

www.lapiccoladeli.com

HERBS

Jekka's Herb Farm

Jekka's Herb Farm boasts the largest collection of culinary herbs in the UK

www.jekkasherbfarm.com

Seeds of Italy

A family-run business since 1783. Suppliers of high-quality herb, tomato and vegetable seeds, as well as Italian seasonings, coffee and olive oil.

www.seedsofitaly.com

MEAT

In our restaurants, the wholesalers we use are Duke's Hill in Yorkshire for ham and Country Butcher in Gloucestershire for pork – names that are worth looking out for for in delis and shops selling meat products. And don't forget to ask your butcher for hog casing, or try these suppliers:

www.weschenfelder.co.uk

www.sausagemaking.org

Brindisa

Suppliers of cured ham, salami and sausages to Franco Manca restaurants.

www.brindisa.com

Ginger Pig

Suppliers of excellent meat to Franco Manca restaurants, with five London butchery shops.

www.thegingerpig.co.uk

INDEX

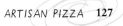

ACKNOWLEDGEMENTS

Giuseppe and Bridget are both grateful to culinary figureheads from their pasts. In Giuseppe's case, the Neopolitan family kitchen was presided over by Geraldina Sepalone, his father's cook, who introduced him to the art of pizza and cooking in general. Bridget's baking inspiration was characterised by her grandmother, Lottie Dicks, who lived on a farm in a remote rural outpost in South Africa, where little could be bought and most things were made from scratch. In addition, both the authors would like to thank Marco Parente for his fundamental advice on dough, and Sita Devi for cleaning up after our mess while we were experimenting at home.

Disclaimer: *The information contained in this book is intended as a general guide. The curing recipes are based on the authors' own experimentation and research and neither the publisher nor the authors can be held responsible for the consequences of the application or misapplication of any of the information or ideas presented in this book.*

Published in Great Britain in 2013 by Kyle Books, an imprint of Octopus Publishing Group Ltd
Carmelite House
50 Victoria Embankment
London EC4Y 0DZ
www.kylebooks.co.uk

ISBN: 978–085783–217–7

10 9 8

Giuseppe Mascoli & Bridget Hugo are hereby identified as the author of this work in accordance with section 77 of Copyright, Designs and Patents Act 1988.

Photography: Philip Webb
Design: Carl Hodson
Prop styling: Polly Webb Wilson
Food styling: Rosie Reynolds
Project editor: Judith Hannam
Editor: Vicki Murrell
Production: Nic Jones and David Hearn

A CIP record for this title is available from the British Library.

Printed and bound in Italy

MIX
Paper from responsible sources
FSC® C104740